Contents

Creating 6-Trait Revisers and Editors for Grade 2

30 Revision and Editing Lessons

Vicki Spandel

Writer in Residence, Great Source Education Group

PEARSON

Boston   New York   San Francisco
Mexico City   Montreal   Toronto   London   Madrid   Munich   Paris
Hong Kong   Singapore   Tokyo   Cape Town   Sydney

Thank you to the following individuals for reviewing this book.
Rachel Shreve, Brooks Elementary School
Rhea D. Vytlacil, Fox Ridge Elementary School

Executive Editor: Aurora Martínez Ramos
Editorial Assistant: Kara Kikel
Executive Marketing Manager: Krista Clark
Marketing Manager: Danae April
Production Editor: Janet Domingo
Editorial-Production Service: Kathy Smith
Composition Buyer: Linda Cox
Manufacturing Buyer: Megan Cochran
Interior Design and Composition: Schneck-DePippo Graphics
Photo Researcher: Schneck-DePippo Graphics
Cover Administrator: Linda Knowles

For related titles and support materials, visit our online catalog at www.allynbaconmerrill.com.

Between the time website information is gathered and then published, it is not unusual for some sites to have closed. Also, the transcription of URLs can result in typographical errors. The publisher would appreciate notification where these errors occur so that they may be corrected in subsequent editions.

ISBN-13: 978-0-205-58100-9   ISBN-10: 0-205-58100-5

Printed in the United States of America
10 9 8 7 6 5 4 3 2 1 Bind-Rite 12 11 10 09 08

**Allyn & Bacon
is an imprint of**

www.allynbaconmerrill.com

Creating Revisers and Editors

Welcome!

. . . to a series of revision and editing lessons designed to complement and extend instructional ideas found in *Creating Young Writers* (for grades K through 3). These lessons offer students an opportunity to learn and practice revision and editing skills by working with text that is *not their own*, and then extend what they have learned by using those same strategies to strengthen their own writing. They are designed to let students have fun even as they gain skills on which they will build throughout their writing lives.

Focused Revision = Strong Revisers

Most teachers tell me that revision is the most difficult part of the writing process to teach. I agree. Revision is difficult to teach—and to *do*. Writers need practice revising, and working with someone else's text allows beginning writers to "play" with writing in a very safe way because the results need not be assessed (except in the sense that you may wish to check to see that they are done). Also, it is not their own work under the spotlight.

But wait—aren't second graders too young to revise?

They are indeed—if we think of revision as handing them back their own drafts and saying, "Please revise this for tomorrow." This makes about as much sense as handing them the keys to the car and saying, "Take me to the airport, would you?"

But if we re-define revision as "taking another look," or "reflecting on the writing" or "finding another way to say it," we find that second graders are not only ready, but very good at it. Anyone who has worked with second graders knows that they love to share their opinions—when we are really interested in hearing them. They also love to brainstorm solutions to problems. Problem solving turns revision into a game—one in which everyone can participate because they will not need pencils in their hands every moment.

With beginners, it is also critical to keep the revision task small—and focused. Asking second grade students to revise whole pieces of writing—or even to recopy them—is a recipe for ensuring that most of them will wind up disliking revision and even the writing process itself. That is just the opposite of what we want.

My purpose is to help students build a repertoire of revision and editing skills, each one very manageable for a young, independent writer. We make revision and editing *possibilities* visible when we share samples of writing, talk about them, and use them as models. "This," we say, "is how one writer puts detail into her writing," or "Here is one interesting way a writer found to start a sentence. Do you think we could make a sentence like this one?" The more possibilities writers see, the better they get at revision.

All lessons are trait-connected.

The lessons in this collection are all trait-based, all connected to features within a given trait. For example, students may come up with a new ending (in relation to the trait of organization) or combine two sentences (in relation to the trait of sentence fluency).

The lessons offer students a hands-on approach to writing, teaching specific strategies that take the mystery out of writing and revising. Trait-based writing and revision teaches student writers to *think like readers*, and this is precisely what makes revision work.

> Please note that these lessons are a perfect complement to your own instruction or any materials, such as the *Write Traits Classroom Kits* (by Vicki Spandel and Jeff Hicks) that you may use to teach *ideas, organization, voice, word choice, sentence fluency,* and *conventions.*

What are the six traits of writing?

Here is a quick overview that not only describes the traits, but sums up what to look for in the writing of second graders:

Trait 1

Ideas

Ideas are the heart of the message: the writer's main point or storyline together with all the details that help make it clear and vivid for the reader.

At Primary Level

At primary level, ideas show up as a clear message, a strong main idea, details in text or in drawings, or clear labels.

Trait 2

Organization

Organization is the overall design or structure of the writing, including the lead (or beginning), the flow of ideas, the transitions connecting those ideas, and the conclusion (ending).

At Primary Level

At primary level, organization shows up as coordination between text and drawing, sequencing (through text or pictures), use of titles and labels, use of "The End" or a conclusion, a progression of ideas or pattern of some sort (comparison, problem-solution, first to last), or use of words that help a reader make connections: *Next, Then, Later, One day, When it was over, When I got home, Then, However, Because* and so on.

Trait 3

Voice

Voice is the writer's unique way of expressing ideas—the general sound and tone of the piece, the link between writer and reader, the verbal fingerprints of the writer on the paper.

At Primary Level

At primary level, voice shows up as a unique or highly individual style or approach; emotion, passion, enthusiasm for a topic; text that makes a reader laugh, cry, get the chills, or recall a personal connection; text readers want to share aloud; or any feature that makes the reader say, "This piece HAS to have come from this student."

Trait 4

Word Choice

Word choice includes all the individual words as well as phrases and expressions the writer uses to convey ideas and feelings.

At Primary Level

At primary level, word choice shows up as use of precise words, action words, new words, unusual or striking expressions, words that convey sensory detail—and the right word at the right moment: "I was devastated" (as one second grader wrote when her grandfather died).

Trait 5

Sentence Fluency

Sentence fluency is the flow and rhythm of language, variety in sentences, a natural sound, and the degree to which text can be read with expression and voice.

At Primary Level

At primary level, fluency begins with *use of sentences,* period—then extends to use of multiple sentences, variety in sentence beginnings, use of longer sentences (resulting from the combination of two main thoughts), use of dialogue, and use of fragments (*Wow! Oh, boy!*), or repetition (*It snowed and snowed*) for effect.

Trait 6

Conventions

Conventions involve anything a copy editor would take care of to make text easier to process, including (but not limited to) spelling, punctuation, grammar and usage, capitalization, paragraphing, spacing, and layout.

At Primary Level

At primary level, conventions include things we often take for granted with older writers, such as spacing between words, use of margins, centering a title on the page, directionality of letters, writing left to right, and wrapping sentences (dropping down and left to begin a new line). Conventions also include stylistic preferences, such as using a period instead of an exclamation point.

What if I have not worked with the six traits before?

Even if you do not use trait-based instructional materials, you will find this revision and editing practice very student and teacher friendly. If you are not *at all* familiar with the Six Traits of Writing, however, I urge you to read *Creating Young Writers*, second edition (2008, Pearson Education) prior to using these lessons. Remember that the lessons are an extension of that text. The text itself offers numerous examples and descriptions that will help you understand:

- What the six traits are.
- How they look in primary writing.
- How to use trait language in coaching your second graders.

The text will also provide you with rubrics, checklists, and numerous ideas for introducing traits to students.

How are the lessons in *Creating Revisers and Editors, Grade 2,* set up?

In this collection, you will find **15 conventions** (editing) lessons and **15 revision** lessons, three revision lessons for each of the first five traits: ideas, organization, voice, word choice, and sentence fluency.

The revision lessons emphasize:

- Sharing of literature.
- Modeling by the teacher.
- Working in pairs.
- Revision followed by discussion.

Each lesson is designed to be completed within roughly **30–35 minutes**. All are designed for use with second grade writers and revisers. If you find a lesson is difficult for some students, you can adjust the amount of revising they do. You can also break a lesson into two parts (or even more). For example, you may wish to do the introduction and group revision one day, followed by the individual revision (with partners' support) the next day.

Students will work with classmates or partners most of the time. When they work individually, they will have a chance to check their work with a partner. This provides discussion opportunities for students who are skilled—and a safety net for students who are challenged.

In each lesson, students have several opportunities to practice *one kind of skill*, such as adding detail. A struggling writer may make one or two small revisions in a given sample. Students who are ready for a bigger challenge can make several revisions—and then go on to apply the skill as they draft an original piece of writing. Feel free to adapt the lessons in this way as needed.

Lesson Format and Presentation

Each revision lesson contains the following components:

- Introduction
- Quotation or sample from literature
- Models A and B for discussion (one strong, one problematic)
- A suggested revision of the weaker model
- A blackline master for Whole Class Revision (Sample C)
- A suggested revision of the Whole Class Revision piece
- A blackline master for Revision Practice with Partners (Sample D)
- A suggested revision of Sample D

Preparing for the Lesson. To prepare for the lesson, you should make one copy of each blackline master for each student in the class—and for yourself, if you wish to make notes. You may also wish to make an overhead transparency copy of Samples C and D (to use for modeling revision).

Introducing the Lesson. Each revision lesson begins with (1) a short introduction describing the focus of the lesson, and (2) a brief sample from literature or professional writing to help you illustrate an important writing feature: e.g., *details involving sounds*. (If you have access to the literature from which the sample is taken, you may wish to have it handy for later use with students, so you can share additional examples.)

Teaching the Lesson. After introducing the lesson, remind students that you will focus on *one kind* of revision strategy. Then, follow these steps:

- Pass out copies of Samples A and B.
- Read each sample aloud as students follow along, and discuss strengths and problems, asking students which sample is stronger and what they might do to revise the weaker sample (**4 minutes**).
- Optional: Share our suggested revision of the weaker sample (**2 minutes**).
- Pass out Sample C (*Whole Class Revision*).
- Read the Whole Class Revision text aloud as students follow along OR ask a student to read it aloud as others follow (**1 minute**).
- Invite students to work with partners in identifying problems with Sample C, making notes they will use to *coach you* (**3 minutes**).
- Invite students (as a class) to coach you as you work through a revision of Sample C on the overhead or whiteboard (**4 minutes,** including discussion). Read your revision aloud to close this part of the lesson.

Day 1 ends here, if you split the lesson.

- Refresh students' memories about the focus of the revision lesson. Place your Whole Class Revision back on the overhead, and (if you wish), compare the changes you and your students have made with our suggested revision for Sample C (**3 minutes**).

- Pass out Sample D (*Revision Practice with Partners*).

- Ask students to revise Sample D *independently*, then to check with their partners to compare strategies and results (**5 minutes**).

- Ask two or three pairs of students to share their revisions. The goal is to hear some variations, despite use of parallel strategies (**3–4 minutes**).

- Optional: Compare your revisions to our suggested revision of Sample D (**3 minutes**).

What if our revisions do not agree with the suggested text?

In most cases, your *editing* (capitals, periods, question marks) should agree very closely with our suggestions for corrected copy. Admittedly, though, even handbooks do not all agree on every issue, so I recommend choosing one handbook to be your final authority, and in the case of any disagreement, consult that handbook. My suggestion: *Write Source: The New Generation* (for Grade 2). 2006. Published by Great Source Education.

With *revision* lessons, of course (adding detail, changing a title, combining two sentences), there are no "correct" answers. What matters is that you and your students identify problems within the text and revise them in a way that makes the writing more clear and readable. The suggested revisions are intended to guide you, to make you aware of possibilities, and to increase your comfort in modeling revision with your students. They are not meant to restrict what you can or should do as writers and revisers.

How are revision and editing different?

Revision involves re-seeing and re-thinking a piece. Are the ideas clear? How does it begin and end? How does it flow? Does this voice speak to my readers?

Editing affects clarity, certainly—but in a slightly different way. Editorial decisions involve spelling, punctuation, grammar, spacing, layout, and everything that makes a document pleasing to the eye and easy to process as a reader.

It is certainly possible to edit and revise at the same time; professional writers do this. However, if we teach it as one big step, we run the risk that students will think they are revising when they correct faulty spelling or change verb tense. Revision is bigger and deeper than this.

Editing lesson format. The editing lessons have two parts: (1) introduction of the editing focus for that lesson (e.g., inserting missing words), and (2) practice text that allows students to practice just that focus strategy without having to look for or correct other kinds of errors.

Students do not correct a given problem just one time. They correct it several times or more. With repetition, an editorial response becomes second nature. Asking students to focus on just one thing at a time helps ensure that they will receive enough practice to think and work like editors—and thus allow those skills to carry over into their own writing. Cumulative lessons give students a chance to combine and practice several editorial skills. Because some lessons in this set are cumulative, I recommend *teaching the editing lessons in order.*

Note
Any lessons from this set can be repeated at any time, and you may wish to repeat some editing lessons several times during the year.

What are the "Next Steps"?

The Next Steps at the close of each revision lesson suggest ways that students can extend and reinforce their learning by applying the skills and strategies of that lesson to their own work. The Next Steps also include suggested instructional activities or strategies for students who need a challenge.

How do these lessons fit into a writing workshop?

These revision and editing lessons are bigger than what is commonly called a "minilesson" or "focused lesson," but they are much smaller than a writing assignment or project, and are not meant to take the place of personal writing. Rather, they are meant to serve as a stepping stone between learning a trait and applying the features within that trait to one's own work. For this reason, they work as a perfect complement to any other trait-based instructional materials you may be using. Further, because they are specifically designed to help students become independent editors and revisers, they fit very well into any writing workshop format that stresses a process approach. Here are two examples:

Example One

Suppose your students are writing stories. One key to a good story is a good ending. You might choose to do the lesson on endings before students write their stories—and then simply use it as a reminder: "Do you remember how many of you said you liked surprise endings—something you weren't expecting? We came up with a good surprise ending when you were coaching me yesterday. You might think about surprises as you write today."

Example Two

Let's say your students have done some descriptive writing and have drafts in their folders. You decide to do the word choice lesson that asks students to brainstorm alternatives to the overused word *nice*. After completing the lesson (later that same day or the next day), you might say, "We did a pretty good job of coming up with words writers can use instead of *nice*. Let's take a look at the descriptions we wrote to see if any of us used the word *nice*—and if we did, let's think about finding another word to make our writing stronger."

You can strengthen this very small revision extension by:

- Simply asking students to delete the word *nice* and insert an alternative on the line above, using a caret (no need to rewrite the draft!).

- Encouraging students to share their revisions with partners and to ask for suggestions.

- Checking a sample of your own work and making a change in something you have written—and then sharing your revision with students.

What other things can I do to make these lessons more effective?

- Read *Creating Young Writers*, second edition (Pearson Education), and keep a copy handy to refer to as you use these lessons (www.allynbaconmerrill.com).

- Don't plan to revise or assess *everything* students create. It will be overwhelming for both them and you. Give them lots of writing time, use the lessons to "play" with revision, and allow them to choose an occasional draft of their own to revise. (They will learn and apply many strategies even without prompting from you.)

- Ask students to keep drafts in a folder so that if and when you do wish to try revision on a personal piece, they know where to look.

- Keep revision very, *very* small for second graders. Changing one word or inserting one detail is often enough—unless the student chooses to do more. Do not require re-copying. Think of revision as "playing with the writing."

- Ask students to double space drafts, and to leave large side margins, providing plenty of room to insert a word or phrase should they wish to do so.

- Write with your students, and model the kinds of things you would like them to do, such as double spacing copy—or inserting a word or phrase you think of later—or changing a title because you've thought of one you like better.

- Describe revision as "changing your mind"—not "fixing." It is like doing your hair a different way or changing your shirt or deciding to have something different for lunch. Revision is a choice, not a penalty for doing it wrong.

- Seat students in such a way that working in pairs is easy and comfortable.

- Provide any auxiliary materials they might find useful: word lists, illustrated dictionaries, checklists, special pens or pencils for editing and revising, and so on.

- Provide additional examples of various writing features from the literature you share with your students. One brief example is provided in each lesson, but the more samples you provide, the more clear it becomes how writing looks when it is working well. **A bibliography of all books referenced in these lessons** appears at the end of this introduction.

- Practice modeling so that it feels natural and so that you are comfortable interweaving the tasks of reading copy (from an overhead or whiteboard), asking questions of your students, and using their suggestions to create revised or edited copy. Models are provided, so there is nothing for you to invent—unless you wish to do so. (If you and your students come up with a better way to revise a sample, by all means *go with it*—our sample is only one suggestion.) When you model, with students coaching you, you allow them to see their thinking in concrete form. You bring their revision to life. This gives them confidence to try a second revision on their own.

Checklists

Creating Revisers and Editors, Grade 2

Note to the Teacher

Following is a series of checklists intended for use with this set of lessons. Use the checklists *one at a time*, as you are teaching the lessons for a particular trait. For example, as you work on the lessons for the trait of ideas, share the Ideas Checklist with students and encourage them to use it when revising (or just taking a quick look at) their own work. After you teach the lessons for another trait, share the checklist for *that trait*. In this way, you gradually add new revision possibilities.

Keeping it manageable. Don't expect that second grade students will make revisions to correspond with every item on the checklist. These are just reminders—and if you prefer, you can use them as posters. Also keep in mind that for many young writers, one or two revision tasks at a time may be *plenty*. Part of the power of these lessons is helping beginners see what a big difference even one small change—a different word, a single detail—can make.

How is a checklist different from a writing guide? A Writing Guide (which does not appear in this lesson set) puts features along a continuum, in order to show writers whether their work is at a beginning, mid-point, or strong level. If you want such a continuum for your own assessment purposes, or to use with portfolios, please refer to the primary text for this series, *Creating Writers*, second edition, 2008. (Please note that it is not necessary to use a Writing Guide in conjunction with these lessons.)

Personal Revision Guide

Organization

—— Good title!

—— Interesting beginning

—— Good ending

Personal Revision Guide

Ideas

—— Makes sense

—— Helpful details

—— Sights, sounds, smells

Word Choice

—— New words

—— Action words!

—— Words to make pictures

Voice

—— Feelings!

—— Sounds like ME

—— Special EFFECTS !!! ???

Personal Revision Guide

Conventions

——— Caret (∧) to put in words, punctuation

——— Delete mark (∂) to take things out

——— Spaces between words

——— Capitals to start a sentence

——— Capitals on names

——— Capital "I"

——— No capital in the middle of a word: cAt

——— . ! ?

Personal Revision Guide

Sentence Fluency

——— Different beginnings

——— Small sentences combined

——— Fragments ONLY on purpose!

Bibliography

List of Books Referenced for Grade 2 Lesson Set

Armour, Peter. 1993. *Stop That Pickle!* Boston: Houghton Mifflin.

Arnold, Tedd. 1997. *Parts*. New York: Puffin Books.

Bang, Molly. 1999. *When Sophie Gets Angry—Really, Really Angry*. New York: Scholastic.

Baylor, Byrd. 1977. *Guess Who My Favorite Person Is*. New York: Aladdin Books.

Baylor, Byrd. 1995. *I'm in Charge of Celebrations*. New York: Aladdin.

Brown, Ruth. 1996. *Toad*. New York: Dutton Children's Books.

Cannon, Janell. 2000. *Crickwing*. New York: Harcourt Brace and Company.

Cannon, Janell. 1997. *Verdi*. New York: Harcourt Brace and Company.

Child, Lauren. 2003. *I Am Too Absolutely Small for School*. Cambridge, MA: Candlewick Press.

Cuyler, Margery. 1991. *That's Good! That's Bad!* New York: Henry Holt and Company.

Dahl, Roald. 2007 (reprint edition). *The Twits*. New York: Puffin Books.

Davies, Nicola. 2004. *Bat Loves the Night*. Cambridge, MA: Candlewick Press.

Davies, Nicola. 2001. *Big Blue Whale*. Cambridge, MA: Candlewick Press.

Davies, Nicola. 2003. *Surprising Sharks*. Cambridge, MA: Candlewick Press.

Dowson, Dick. 2004. *Tigress*. Cambridge, MA: Candlewick Press.

Fox, Mem. 1994. *Koala Lou*. New York: Voyager Books.

Fox, Mem. 1998. *Tough Boris*. New York: Voyager Books.

French, Jackie. 2002. *Diary of a Wombat*. New York: Clarion Books.

Hamanaka, Sheila. 1994. *All the Colors of the Earth*. New York: William Morrow and Company.

Jenkins, Steve. 1997. *What Do You Do When Something Wants to Eat You?* Boston: Houghton Mifflin.

Kellogg, Stephen. 2000. *The Missing Mitten Mystery*. New York: Puffin Books.

King-Smith, Dick. 1993. *All Pigs Are Beautiful*. Cambridge, MA: Candlewick Press.

Kramer, Stephen. 1995. *Caves*. Minneapolis: Carolrhoda Books.

Laden, Nina. 1994. *The Night I Followed the Dog*. San Francisco: Chronicle Books.

Lobel, Arnold. 1983. *Mouse Soup*. New York: HarperTrophy.

Lobel, Arnold. 1999. *Frog and Toad Together*. New York: HarperFestival.

Lum, Kate. 1998. *WHAT! CRIED GRANNY: An Almost Bedtime Story*. New York: Puffin Books.

McDermott, Gerald. 1996. *Zomo the Rabbit: A Trickster Tale from West Africa*. New York: Voyager Books.

MacLachlan, Patricia. 1995. *What You Know First*. New York: HarperCollins.

Marshall, James. 1985. *Miss Nelson Is Missing*. Boston: Houghton Mifflin.

Marshall, James. 1997. *George and Martha: The Complete Stories of Two Best Friends*. Boston: Houghton Mifflin.

Mayer, Mercer. 1976. *There's a Nightmare in My Closet*. New York: Puffin Books.

Monks, Lydia. 2004. *Aaaarrgghh! Spider!* Boston: Houghton Mifflin.

Nissenberg, Sandra K. 2002. *The Everything Kids' Cookbook*. Avon, MA: Adams Media Corporation.

Nissenberg, Sandra K. 1998. *I Made It Myself*. Minneapolis: Chronimed Publishing.

Palatini, Margie. 2005. *Bedhead*. New York: Aladdin.

Palatini, Margie. 2006. *Oink?* New York: Simon & Schuster.

Paulsen, Gary. 1994. *Dogteam*. New York: Dragonfly Books.

Pritcher, Caroline. 2004. *Lord of the Forest*. London: Frances Lincoln Children's Books.

Radunsky, Vladamir. 2004. *What does peace look like?* New York: Atheneum Books.

Rogers, Judi. 1996. *Fun With Kids in the Kitchen Cookbook*. Hagerstown, MD: Review and Herald Publishing Association.

Rylant, Cynthia. 1985. *The Relatives Came*. New York: Aladdin Books.

Simon, Seymour. 2001. *Animals Nobody Loves*. New York: Random House.

Steig, William. 1971. *Amos and Boris*. New York: Puffin Books.

Steig, William. 1982. *Dr. DeSoto*. New York: Farrar, Straus and Giroux.

Steptoe, Javaka, illustrator. Individual poets. 1997. *In Daddy's Arms I Am Tall: African Americans Celebrating Fathers*. New York: Lee and Low Books.

Stevens, Janet. 2005. *The Great Fuzz Frenzy*. New York: Harcourt Brace and Company.

Van Allsburg, Chris. 1985. *The Polar Express*. Boston: Houghton Mifflin.

Wallace, Karen. 2002. *Gentle Giant Octopus*. Cambridge, MA: Candlewick Press.

Wallace, Karen. 1998. *Tale of a Tadpole*. New York: DK Publishing.

White, E. B. 1952 (renewed 1980). *Charlotte's Web*. New York: HarperCollins.

Wilkes, Angela. 2007. *The Usborne First Cookbook*. London: Usborne Publishing.

Willems, Mo. 2006. *Don't Let the Pigeon Stay Up Late*. New York: Hyperion Books for Children.

Willems, Mo. 2004. *Knuffle Bunny*. New York: Hyperion Books for Children.

Lessons for Grade 2

Indicates editing lesson.

Using the Caret (^) to Insert Information

Trait Connection: **Being an Editor (Conventions)**

Introduction (Share with students in your own words)

The caret looks like a small arrow (^). Putting in a caret is like pointing a finger. It says, "Put some information right here." That information might be a missing word—or a new detail. Here is an example:

Ali and Jon to the soccer game.

There's a word missing from this sentence. Can you tell what it is? If you said something like *went*, you're right. Here's how an editor can use a caret to put this word in *without writing the sentence over*:

went
Ali and Jon ^ to the soccer game.

Writers can also use the caret to add detail, like this:

on a river raft
Jamal and Elli took a thrilling ride. ^

Teaching the Lesson (General Directions for Teachers)

1. Show students what the caret (^) looks like.

2. Practice writing a caret and using it to insert a word or detail—with our examples or ones you make up. Write with your students.

3. Share the editing lesson on the following page. Read it aloud *exactly as written*. Notice that the ONLY errors in this lesson are *missing words*. Students may insert any word that makes sense. (The corrected copy offers suggestions.) They may also add details—*but they do not need to*.

4. Ask them to work individually first, then check with a partner. Remind them that there are *3 words missing*.

5. When everyone is done, ask them to *coach you* as you edit the copy on an overhead transparency.

6. When you finish, check your editing against the corrected copy on page 20.

Editing Goal: Use Carets (^) to fill in 3 missing words.
Next, look for missing words in your own work.

Editing Practice

Use the caret (∧)
Find 3 missing words.

Ben and Juli went out for pizza. Ben wanted

peppers, but Juli olives. They decided to get

peppers one side, and olives on the other

side. They both happy!

Corrected Copy

3 missing words inserted

Ben and Juli went out for pizza. Ben wanted

wanted

peppers, but Juli ˄ olives. They decided to get

on

peppers ˄ one side, and olives on the other

were

side. They ˄ both happy!

Revising with a "Close-Up"

Trait Connection: **Ideas**

Introduction

If you wanted to take a picture of a flower, how close would you stand? A mile away? Of course not! How about fifty feet? Still too far? How about two feet? That's more like it. When you move in close, you can see more. You see little things, like how the color on the petals changes from yellow to orange, or how one leaf has been munched by a caterpillar, or how there's a ladybug crawling right over the center of the flower. Those little things—called details—make photographs more interesting. They make writing more interesting, too.

Teacher's Sidebar . . .

You are not really creating a snapshot every time you write. But pretending you *are* can help you zero in on the same kinds of details you would look for through your camera lens.

Focus and Intent

This lesson is intended to help students:

- Think about the concept of "detail".
- Listen for detail in writing that is shared aloud.
- Add the same kinds of details in writing that a photographer looks for in shooting a picture.

Teaching the Lesson

Step 1: Introducing Photographic Detail

Ask students to fold an 8 ½ x 11 sheet of paper in half, then in half again, so it is one-quarter size. (*Do this with them so you can model as you go.*) After the paper is folded, cut a tiny square out of the inside corner by cutting one-half inch each way. Discard the cut-out and open the paper. You should have a one-inch-square hole right in the center. Ask students to look for "photographer's details" by peering through this hole. It's interesting how many "small" details pop out at you. List a few with your students, for example:

- The toe of a shoe
- My thumb
- My friend's eyebrow

- A crack in the floor
- A spider on the wall

Step 2: Making the Reading-Writing Connection

Share the following example, or a favorite of your own. In this passage, author Nicola Davies takes us right up next to a blue whale. Read the description (twice if you wish); then, ask students to name the details they hear as you read—and to think how different the description would be if the author were describing the whale from shore—or from an airplane window.

Example

Look into its eye. It's as big as a teacup and as dark as the deep sea. Just behind the eye is a hole as small as the end of a pencil. The hole is one of the blue whale's ears—sticking out ears would get in the way when the whale is swimming.

(Nicola Davies, *Big Blue Whale*. 2001. Cambridge, MA: Candlewick Press, page 9.)

Step 3: Involving Students as Evaluators

Ask students to look at Samples A and B as you read them aloud, specifically look-ing and listening for a photographer's details: What takes us right up close and makes each piece interesting? Have students work with a partner, and when you finish read-ing, give them a minute to highlight details in each example that stand out.

Discussing Results

Most students should find Sample B significantly stronger. Discuss differences between A and B, asking students to tell you what specific details work in Sample B. Also ask what the writer could add to Sample A that would take readers in for a "close-up."

Step 4: Modeling Revision

- Share Sample C (*Whole Class Revision*) with students. Read it aloud.
- Ask students if this writer has brought readers in for a "close-up" yet. (Most should say *no*.)
- With students' help, identify one or two possibilities for creating close-up details. Talk about which ones will create the most vivid "snapshot."
- Using students' suggestions, revise the draft. Use carets (^) to insert new details.
- When you finish, read your whole class revision aloud. (You may com-pare your revised version with our suggestion—but this is an optional step. Your copy need not match ours in any way.)

Step 5: Revising with Partners

Share Sample D (*Revising with Partners*). Read it aloud as students follow along. Then, ask students to follow the basic steps you modeled with Sample C. *Working with partners,* they should:

- Talk about whether the writer takes readers in for a "close-up"—or not.
- Talk about one or two close-up details they could add.
- Revise by using a caret (^) to insert new details.
- Read their revision aloud.

Step 6: Sharing and Discussing Results

When students have finished, ask several pairs of students to share their revisions aloud with the whole class. As a group, discuss the kinds of changes they have made. Emphasize the vividness of close-up details, and discuss how this helps create a snapshot in the reader's mind.

Next Steps

- Remind students to *double space* their own drafts just in case they ever wish to add a close-up detail later.

- Model the addition of one close-up detail to a piece of your own writing. Ask students for suggestions if you wish. Then (optional), if they seem ready, invite them to look at a piece of their own writing and ask themselves whether they wish to add a close-up detail. They should work with partners on this—and should not feel pressured to add details unless they wish to do so.

- Listen for close-up details in any literature you share.
  Recommended:
  - *Big Blue Whale* by Nicola Davies. 2001. Cambridge, MA: Candlewick Press.
  - *Gentle Giant Octopus* by Karen Wallace. 2002. Cambridge, MA: Candlewick Press.
  - *Guess Who My Favorite Person Is* by Byrd Baylor. 1977. New York: Aladdin Books.
  - *The Relatives Came* by Cynthia Rylant. 1985. New York: Aladdin Books.

- Take your one-inch "snapshot" paper lenses to another site—perhaps the playground (or even ask students to take them home). Make a class list of close-up details your writers see. Invite them to use any of those close-up details as a basis for a descriptive paragraph.

- *For students who need a challenge:* Invite students to use actual close-up photographs (their own or someone else's) to accompany a piece of descriptive writing.

Sample A

Two goldfish circled around

the fish tank. One was very big

and swam slowly. The other one

was tiny but swam fast.

Sample B

The fat black spider found a cozy spot in a sunny window. She sent out long strands of sticky silk that clung to the rough wood. Working fast, she shaped a lacy web with her hairy black legs. A curious fly inched his way toward the web—coming closer, closer. His shiny fly eyes rolled this way and that. In the center of the web, the spider crouched very still, waiting.

Suggested Revision of Sample A

Two goldfish circled around

almost three inches long

the fish tank. One was ~~very~~

with huge golden fins and bulging eyes. He

~~big and~~ swam slowly. The

zipped around the tank like

other one ~~was tiny but swam~~

a one-inch black rocket.

~~fast~~

Sample C: Whole Class Revision

My cousin Ari's room was

quite a mess. There were

lots of toys on the floor.

There was even some old

food under the bed.

Sample D: Revising with Partners

A dog followed Becca down

the road to her grandma's

house. When Becca went in,

the dog looked at her through

the screen door.

Suggested Revisions of C and D

Sample C: Whole Class Revision

My cousin Ari's room was

quite a mess. There were

baseballs, Legos, and arms and legs from action figures

~~lots of toys~~ on the floor.

a week-old plate of nachos

There was even ~~some old~~

unmade, lumpy

~~food~~ under the bed.

Sample D: Revising with Partners

big, scruffy, yellow

A dog followed Becca down

the road to her grandma's

house. When Becca went in,

with sad brown eyes, and poked

the dog looked at her ~~through~~

his wet black nose right against

the screen door.

Using the Delete Mark (⌀) to Cross Out Repeated Words

Trait Connection: **Being an Editor (Conventions)**

Introduction (Share with students in your own words)

The delete mark looks like a line with a curl at the end (⌀). A delete mark says, "Take this out." The something to take out could be an extra word the writer repeated by accident:

> Marin and Angel went went swimming.

Which word is repeated? If you said *went*, you have a good editor's ear and eye. Here's how an editor can use a delete mark to take out the extra word *without writing the sentence over:*

> Marin and Angel ~~went~~ went swimming.

Writers sometimes change their minds about how to say something. A delete mark and caret together make this kind of change easy:

> Marin and Angel ~~went~~ took off at dawn to go swimming.

Teaching the Lesson (General Guidelines for Teachers)

1. Show students what the delete mark (⌀) looks like.
2. Practice writing the delete mark and using it to take out a repeated word or make a change—using our examples or ones you make up. Be sure to write with your students.
3. Share the editing lesson on the following page. Read it aloud *exactly as written*. Notice that the ONLY errors in this lesson are *repeated words*. Students should delete one word in each repeated set. They do not *need* to make any other changes (but they can play with the wording if they wish).
4. Ask them to work individually first, then check with a partner. Remind them that they are looking for *3 repeated words*.
5. When everyone is done, ask them to *coach you* as you edit the copy on an overhead transparency.
6. When you finish, check your editing against the corrected copy.

Editing Goal: Use delete marks (⌀) to delete 3 repeated words.
Next, look for repeated words in your own work.

Editing Practice

Use the delete mark (ℓ)
Find 3 repeated words.

A fuzzy caterpillar was was crawling up the flower,

gripping the stem with his small feet. He took one

tiny nibble of a a leaf, and then moved on. Maybe

the the leaf was too bitter!

Corrected Copy

3 repeated words

A fuzzy caterpillar was ~~was~~ crawling up the flower,

gripping the stem with his small feet. He took one

tiny nibble of a ~~a~~ leaf, and then moved on. Maybe

the ~~the~~ leaf was too bitter!

Revising by Listening

Trait Connection: **Ideas**

Introduction

Have you ever been so quiet that you thought you could hear your own heart beating? Now, *that's* quiet! Writers who pay attention to their surroundings may notice sounds others would not. Shhh . . . listen. What do you hear *right now?* If you wrote about those sounds, your readers could feel as if they were right in the room with you—hearing all the things you hear.

Teacher's Sidebar . . .

Many people have experienced the sounds of a busy classroom or city street. But sounds are important even in places that seem quiet. When you *really* listen, you might hear a bird hopping on a rooftop, a clock ticking, a mouse crawling behind a wall—or your own heart beating. It's often the *soft* sounds, the *less noticed* sounds, that make for good writing.

Focus and Intent

This lesson is intended to help students:

- Think of "detail" in terms of sound.
- Listen for details of sound in writing that is shared aloud.
- Use memory, experience, and imagination to add details of sound in revising, and then in their own original descriptive writing.

Teaching the Lesson

Step 1: Introducing Details of Sound

Humans are such visual creatures that we may not even notice sounds when our eyes are taking in too many details. Ask students to close their eyes or even blindfold themselves for two minutes of careful listening. Ask everyone to be very quiet during this experiment—no shuffling feet, no talking or laughing. You can do this in your classroom, or in any nearby environment (gym, lunchroom, hallway, playground). If possible, take students outside to listen to sounds you won't hear indoors. Discuss and record what you hear that you might not have noticed before—such as:

- Echoes of far-off laughter, coughing, or talking

- Whispers

- Breathing

- Wind blowing

- Leaves rustling

- Birds chirping

- Traffic sounds

- Bells ringing

Note

If you have auditorally challenged students, you can ask them to use both imagination and heightened awareness to describe the world as *they* hear it. They may weave in other sensory details, such as sense of touch. They can also share (with you and other students) ways that they have learned to recognize sounds they may not "hear" in a conventional way—sounds other listeners may not even be sensitive to.

Step 2: Making the Reading-Writing Connection

Share the following example, or a favorite of your own. In this passage, teacher and scientific researcher Stephen Kramer takes us inside a place many people have never visited: a dark cave. Just how quiet *is* it inside? Think about the author's use of the word "whisper." Is this a good choice to describe the water inside a cave? Why?

Example

When you sit quietly in a cave, surrounded on all sides by solid rock, time seems to stand still. The air is so quiet you can hear your heart beat. Drops of falling water whisper in the darkness, just as they have for thousands of years.

(Stephen Kramer, *Caves*. 1995. Minneapolis, MN: Carolrhoda Books, Inc., page 38.)

Step 3: Involving Students as Evaluators

Ask students to look at Samples A and B as you read them aloud, specifically looking and listening for details of sound: What sounds are so vivid that they make us feel as if we are right there with the writer? Have students work with a partner, and when you finish reading, give them a minute to highlight their favorite details from either example.

Discussing Results

Most students should find Sample A significantly stronger. Discuss differences between A and B, asking students to tell you what specific details of sound they notice in Sample A. Also ask what the writer *could* add to Sample B to create some details of sound. (If you wish, following your discussion, share our suggested revision of Sample B.)

Step 4: Modeling Revision

- Share Sample C (*Whole Class Revision*) with students. Read it aloud.
- Ask students if this writer has included important details of sound. (Most should say *no*.)
- With students' help, identify one or two possibilities for sharing details of sound with the reader.
- Using students' suggestions, revise the draft. Use carets (^) to insert new details.
- When you finish, read your class revision aloud. (You may compare your revised version with ours—this is an optional step. Your copy *need not match ours in any way*.)

Step 5: Revising with Partners

Share Sample D (*Revising with Partners*). Read it aloud as students follow along. Then, ask students to follow the basic steps you modeled with Sample C. *Working with partners,* they should:

- Talk about whether the writer uses effective details of sound—or not.
- Talk about one or two sounds they could add.
- Revise by using a caret (^) to insert new details. (It is also fine to cross out any words they do not need.)
- Read their revision aloud.

Step 6: Sharing and Discussing Results

When students have finished, ask several pairs of students to share their revisions aloud with the whole class. As a group, have students discuss the kinds of changes they have made. Emphasize the value of sound in putting the reader right at the scene.

Next Steps

- Remind students to *double space* their own drafts just in case they wish to add details later. (This is a *reminder*—not a requirement.)
- Model the addition of sound to a piece of your own descriptive writing. Ask students for suggestions as you revise, letting them watch you make changes.

■ *Optional:* When your students create descriptive or narrative pieces involving place, you may wish to ask them whether they remembered to include details involving sounds—and if not, whether this is something they wish to add.

■ Listen for details of sound in any literature you share.
Recommended:

  ● *Bat Loves the Night* by Nicola Davies. 2004. Cambridge, MA: Candlewick.

  ● *Caves* by Stephen Kramer. 1995. Minneapolis, MN: Carolrhoda Books.

  ● *Charlotte's Web* by E. B. White. 1952. Renewed 1980. New York: HarperCollins.

  ● *Guess Who My Favorite Person Is* by Byrd Baylor. 1977. New York: Aladdin Books.

  ● *Lord of the Forest* by Caroline Pritcher. 2004. London: Frances Lincoln Children's Books.

■ Try listening as a pre-writing strategy when writing to describe a place that your students either have visited or might actually visit: a cafeteria or coffee house, a gym or soccer field, a baby's bedroom, a grocery store, a dog kennel, a zoo or amusement park, a construction site, a hiking trail, bus station, train station, or freeway. Brainstorm the sounds your students notice—or remember. Then write. Remind students that it is not important to capture *every* sound. It is more important to capture one or two sounds that will put the reader right at the scene.

■ *For students who need a challenge:* Expand descriptive skills by asking students to think of an unusual place—one not typically associated with sounds. Examples might be under water, up a tree, in an attic, in a snowbank, under the stairs, or in a garden. What not-so-everyday sounds can they think of to enrich the description?

Sample A

Aunt May was preparing to cook spaghetti.

The large metal pot she'd filled with water was

round on the bottom so it wouldn't sit flat. It

rocked and bumped against the black stovetop.

The water sputtered and gurgled, squirting out

small jets that sizzled as they hit the heat.

Pssst! Sssssssssss . . . Pssssssst! Sssssssssss . . .

Sample B

Many creatures lived in the pond.

Big green frogs hid in the rocks along

the shore. Blackbirds lived in the

cattails. When you walked by, you

could tell the blackbirds were there.

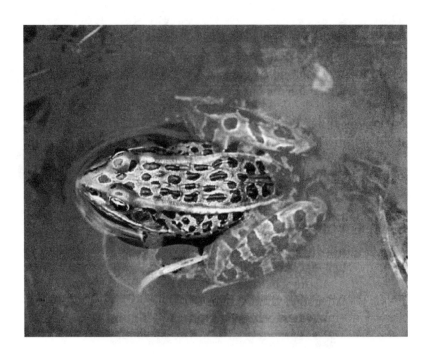

Suggested Revision of Sample B

Many creatures lived in the pond.

Big green frogs hid in the rocks along
croaking in deep voices and plopping into the water.
the shore. Blackbirds lived in the

cattails. When you walked by, you

hear them screeching and fluttering their wings.
could, ~~tell the blackbirds were there~~

Sample C: Whole Class Revision

Toby, a brown mutt with a friendly face, was never a very quiet dog. He made a lot of noise during the day. He even made noise when he slept!

Sample D: Revising with Partners

Lily got separated from her mom at the mall.

Lily was only four, and she was frightened.

She listened hard for her mom's voice, but

she couldn't hear it over the other sounds.

Suggested Revisions of C and D

Sample C: Whole Class Revision

Toby, a brown mutt with a friendly face, was

never a very quiet dog. ~~He made a lot of~~
he barked at people and growled at squirrels.
~~noise~~ During the day, ~~He even made noise~~
he snored and howled and scraped
When he slept, *his claws on the wooden floor,*
pretending he was running.

Sample D: Revising with Partners

Lily got separated from her mom at the mall.

Lily was only four, and she was frightened.

She listened hard for her mom's voice, but

she couldn't hear it over the ~~other~~ sounds
of feet moving, music playing, and
coffee people yelling out orders.

Using the Caret (^) and Pound Sign (#) to Insert Space

Trait Connection: **Being an Editor (Conventions)**

Introduction (Share with students in your own words)

You already know what a caret looks like: ^. It means "Put something here." When you tuck a pound sign inside it, like this— ⚡ —it means "Put space here." This is a very handy sign to know when a writer forgets to leave space between two words, like this:

Nico ranfor cover.

Which two words are run together? If you said *ran* and *for*, you are doing some sharp editing today. Here's how an editor can use the caret and pound sign together to insert a space *without writing the sentence over:*

Nico ranfor cover.

Try another one. Where would you put the caret and pound sign in this sentence?

A bigdog ate my sandwich.

Did you say between *big* and *dog?* That's some fancy editing:

A bigdog ate my sandwich.

Teaching the Lesson (General Guidelines for Teachers)

1. Show students how to write the caret/pound sign combination.
2. Practice using this mark to insert space—with our examples or ones you make up. Be sure to write *with your students.*
3. Share the editing lesson on the following page. Read it aloud *exactly as written.* Notice that the ONLY errors in this lesson are *words run together.*
4. Ask students to work individually first, then check with a partner. Remind them that they need to insert space in *3 sets of words run together.*
5. When everyone is done, ask them to *coach you* as you edit the copy on an overhead transparency.
6. When you finish, check your editing against the corrected copy.

Editing Goal: Use the caret/pound sign to insert space in 3 sets of words. Next, look for run-together words in your own work.

Editing Practice

Use the caret with the pound sign.
Put space between 3 sets of words run together.

The wind was blowing so hard Dav could not keep his

haton. He tried to keep one hand onhis hat. Even so,

thewind almost lifted him right off the ground!

Corrected Copy

3 sets of words split

The wind was blowing so hard Dav could not keep his

haton. He tried to keep one hand onhis hat. Even so,

thewind almost lifted him right off the ground!

Revising with Your Nose

Trait Connection: **Ideas**

Introduction

What does the smell of popcorn make you think of? How about bread or muffins or a cake baking? The earth or sidewalk after a heavy rain? Now let's go in a different direction . . . Have you ever smelled the spray from a skunk? How about a wet dog? A diaper pail? If you're like most people, smells—both good and bad—can take you right back to another time, place, or experience in the blink of an eye. When you weave smells into your writing, you take your reader on a little mental field trip.

Teacher's Sidebar . . .

Mention "skunk," and what do you smell? Right. Mention "paint" and what do you smell? Absolutely! The point is, you don't always have to use the *word* "smell." You don't always have to write about "the *smell* of the skunk" or "the *smell* of fresh paint." Just mentioning the thing itself—*burned toast, burgers grilling, old gym socks*—is usually enough to set the reader's nose a-twitching.

Focus and Intent

This lesson is intended to help students:

- Recognize smells as important details.
- Notice aromatic details in writing that is shared aloud.
- Use memory, experience, and imagination to add aromatic details in revising, and then in their own original descriptive writing.

Teaching the Lesson

Step 1: Introducing Aromatic Details

Smells are powerful. The best way to show this to students is to bring in something for them to smell—and ask what it reminds them of. Popcorn works very well for this, but anything with an intense scent will do (whether pleasant or not): chocolate, candles, fresh mowed grass, fresh cut wood, a leather baseball glove, cut oranges or lemons, herbs of any kind, vanilla, fish oil, alcohol on a cotton swab, planting soil, hay, swamp water in a jar. Choose just two or three (making sure all are safe for students in your class—watch out for allergies!), and after experiencing each scent, ask students to talk (or write) about the memories it brings to mind. How powerful are those memories?

Step 2: Making the Reading-Writing Connection

In *Charlotte's Web,* author E. B. White creates a whole bouquet of smells to describe the barn on Mr. Zuckerman's farm. How many smells do you recognize? Which ones are new? As you listen, think how you would *feel* if you were in this barn right now (smells create mood):

Example

It smelled of hay and it smelled of manure. It smelled of the perspiration of tired horses and the wonderful sweet breath of patient cows . . . It smelled of grain and of harness dressing and of axle grease and of rubber boots and of new rope. And whenever the cat was given a fish-head to eat, the barn would smell of fish.

(E. B. White, *Charlotte's Web.* 1952. Renewed 1980. New York: HarperCollins, page 13.)

Step 3: Involving Students as Evaluators

Ask students to look at Samples A and B as you read them aloud, specifically looking and listening for aromatic details: What mood is created by each piece? Have students work with a partner, and when you finish reading, give them a minute to talk about which sample is stronger.

Discussing Results

Most students should find Sample B significantly stronger. Discuss differences between A and B, asking students to tell you what specific smells the writer includes in Sample B. Also ask what the writer *could* add to Sample A. (If you wish, following your discussion, share our suggested revision of Sample A.)

Step 4: Modeling Revision

- Share Sample C (*Whole Class Revision*) with students. Read it aloud.
- Ask students if this writer has included smells in the description. (Most should say *no.*)
- With students' help, identify one or two smells that could take the reader on a "mental field trip" in this piece.
- Using students' suggestions, revise the draft. Use carets (^) to insert new details. Cross out anything you do not need, using the delete mark (⁄6).
- When you finish, read your class revision aloud. (Optional: Compare your revised version with ours. Your copy *need not match ours in any way.*)

Step 5: Revising with Partners

Share Sample D (*Revising with Partners*). Read it aloud as students follow along. Then, ask students (in pairs) to follow the basic steps you modeled with Sample C. *Working with partners,* they should:

- Talk about whether the writer already includes smells in the writing.

- Talk to each other about the kinds of things Isaac might smell in the old tree fort.

- Revise by adding any details that include smells.

- Read their revision aloud to each other.

Step 6: Sharing and Discussing Results

When students have finished, ask several pairs of students to share their revisions aloud with the whole class. As a group, discuss the kinds of changes they have made. *Note: Tastes* are closely connected to smells. When we taste food, we are *mostly* enjoying the smell. Did any revisers include tastes?

Next Steps

- Remind students to *double space* drafts in case they wish to add details later.

- Model the addition of scents to a piece of your own descriptive writing. Ask students for suggestions as you revise in front of them.

- Using one or more of the scented materials you brought in to introduce the lesson, invite students to write a descriptive or narrative piece weaving in smells. If you share this writing aloud, ask listeners what the smells remind them of—what sort of "field trip" does the writer take them on? How do those smells make them *feel* as they listen? Peaceful? Happy? Excited?

- Listen for aromatic details in any literature you share.
  Recommended:
  - *Charlotte's Web* by E. B. White. 1952. Renewed 1980. New York: HarperCollins.
  - *Guess Who My Favorite Person Is* by Byrd Baylor. 1977. New York: Aladdin Books.
  - *Oink?* by Margie Palatini. 2006. New York: Simon & Schuster.
  - *What Does Peace Feel Like?* by Vladamir Radunsky. 2004. New York: Atheneum Books for Young Readers.

- *For students who need a challenge:* Begin by asking students to think of a place where a person could notice many different smells. Examples might be a zoo, a fair or carnival, a restaurant or deli, a ball park, and so on. Ask them to brainstorm *all* the smells they can think of in connection with that place. Then, using E. B. White's description of the Zuckerman barn as a model, ask them to create a description based *just on smells*.

Sample A

Uncle Ed walked outside and stretched.

He shooed his dog Buck away because

Buck was wet. Then, he filled a big

basket with things from the garden and

took them into the kitchen where Aunt

Liz was cooking something.

Sample B

Sunny thought she could live in the bakery forever. The front case was overflowing with orange muffins, glazed doughnuts, and blackberry scones. On the rack just behind the case sat loaves of fresh bread, still steaming from the oven—rye, whole wheat with sunflower seeds, sourdough—any kind you could think up. In the corner by the woodstove, people laughed, clutching cups of hot chocolate.

Suggested Revision of Sample A

Uncle Ed walked outside and stretched.

He shooed his dog Buck away because

Buck was ~~wet~~ **dripping with water from the duck pond.** Then, he filled a big

basket with ~~things~~ **juicy red tomatoes and fresh corn** from the garden and

took them into the kitchen where Aunt

Liz was cooking ~~something~~ **waffles and bacon.**

Sample C: Whole Class Revision

The old movie house had not been swept

or scrubbed or vacuumed for a long time.

The seats were covered with crumbs. The

floor was piled with trash. Even the carpet

was stained.

Sample D: Revising with Partners

Isaac's tree fort was special to him because
every smell there held a memory. When he
climbed up and poked his head in, Isaac could
smell a whole lot of things.

Suggested Revisions of C and D

Sample C: Whole Class Revision

The old movie house had not been swept

or scrubbed or vacuumed for a long time.

The seats were covered with ~~crumbs.~~ The *bits of stale popcorn.*

floor was piled with ~~trash.~~ Even the carpet *candy wrappers and old gum.*

was stained. *with spilled sodas and sour milk from baby bottles.*

Sample D: Revising with Partners

Isaac's tree fort was special to him because

every smell there held a memory. When he

climbed up and poked his head in, Isaac could

smell ~~a whole lot of things.~~ *the old wool blanket his mom had*

given him, the hot dogs he and his friend Ben always ate in the fort, and the "beachy" smell of his shell collection.

Putting It Together
(Lessons 1, 3, and 5)

Trait Connection: **Being an Editor (Conventions)**

Introduction (Share with students in your own words)

You've had some practice using the caret to put in a missing word, using a delete mark to take out a repeated word, and using a caret and pound sign to put in space when two words are run together. Let's look at some reminder sentences. Then, we'll see if we can put these three editing skills together:

1. Inserting a missing word:

Ryan climbed *the* tree.

2. Deleting a repeated word:

Jesse is my ~~my~~ friend.

3. Inserting space between two words run together:

Watch out for the car.

Teaching the Lesson (General Guidelines for Teachers)

1. Remind students how to write the caret, delete symbol, and caret/pound sign combination.

2. Practice using these marks—with our examples or ones you make up. Be sure to write *with students so they can see you working as an editor.*

3. Share the editing lesson on the following page. Read it aloud *exactly as written.* Notice that there is ONE ERROR OF EACH TYPE in this lesson.

4. Ask students to work individually first, then check with a partner. Remind them that they need to look for *3 errors*: one *missing* word, one *repeated* word, and one set of words *run together.*

5. When everyone is done, ask them to *coach you* as you edit the copy on an overhead transparency.

6. When you finish, check your editing against the corrected copy.

Editing Goals: Finding *three errors*—one *missing* word, one *repeated* word, one example of words *run together.* Being an editor for yourself!

Editing Practice

Find 3 errors.

Aaron built bird house. He hung it in a big elm

tree. In the spring, a bird moved in. In afew weeks,

Aaron heard loud chirping coming from the the

bird house!

Corrected Copy

3 errors corrected

Aaron built _∧ **a** bird house. He hung it in a big elm

tree. In the spring, a bird moved in. In a̲few weeks,

Aaron heard loud chirping coming from the ~~the~~a

bird house!

Revising the Title

Trait Connection: **Organization**

Introduction

Let's play a game. See if you can guess just from the title what a book might be about. Ready? Here goes . . . *Bedhead*. [Pause for responses.] The book *Bedhead* by Margie Palatini is the very funny story of Oliver, whose hair will NOT behave. He and his family try everything—brushing, combing, wetting it down—even gelling it. Nothing seems to work until—well, you'll have to read the book to find *that* out. The point is, titles matter. A good title gets the reader thinking—and guessing what might come next. A *really* good title might even make you want to read a book or story in the first place.

Teacher's Sidebar . . .

Titles take many forms. Some name the most important thing or character in the book—like *Toad* by Ruth Brown or *The Twits* by Roald Dahl. Some refer to an event like *Miss Nelson Is Missing!* by James Marshall or *The Relatives Came* by Cynthia Rylant. Good writers try to think of a title that will get you excited about reading more, and—here's one writer's secret—they often write the title *last*.

Focus and Intent

This lesson is intended to help students:

- Recognize the importance and the function of titles.
- Connect titles to predictions about content.
- Use their imagination and knowledge of the text to come up with a title that is both appealing and appropriate.

Teaching the Lesson

Step 1: Getting Writers Thinking

Titles help us—even *encourage* us—to make predictions about a piece of writing, and also decide whether we would like to read it. This kind of predicting is a game all students can play, for there are no right or wrong answers, *but* (this is the best part) players tend to get better with practice. Gather a set of at least six picture books you have not yet shared with your students (some may be known to a few students, of course) and invite them to make predictions just from the title. Read the titles without showing the cover first. Then, show the cover to see if it provides additional hints. Some can be obvious—others less so. Not-so-obvious books that are fun to share in this way include:

- *I Am Too Absolutely Small for School* by Lauren Child
- *I'm in Charge of Celebrations* by Byrd Baylor
- *The Great Fuzz Frenzy* by Janet Stevens
- *Lord of the Forest* by Caroline Pritcher

After making guesses about content, also ask how many students think this is a book they would like to read.

Step 2: Making the Reading-Writing Connection

Here's a chance to reverse things. This time, you will share a piece of writing *without sharing the title*. In order to make this a real guessing game, you will need to read something your students have not heard previously (and to the extent possible, keep cover and pictures hidden at first). You may choose *anything at all* for this purpose—but here are a few recommendations. For something relatively short and easy, read *any one story* from:

- *Frog and Toad Together* by Arnold Lobel
- *George and Martha* by James Marshall
- *Mouse Soup* by Arnold Lobel

For more of a challenge, you mighty try:

- *Surprising Sharks* by Nicola Davies
- *There's a Nightmare in My Closet* by Mercer Mayer
- *Tough Boris* by Mem Fox

Share the text first. Then, ask students to come up with as many possible titles as they can. When they are finished, share the writer's actual title—which students may or may not prefer to their own!

Step 3: Involving Students as Evaluators

Ask students to look at Samples A and B as you read them aloud, paying attention to the title, and asking whether the title (1) is interesting, and (2) gives them a little clue about what is coming. Have students work with a partner, and when you finish reading each piece, give them a minute to talk about whether the title is a good one—or whether they can come up with something better.

Discussing Results

Discuss differences between A and B, asking students to tell you which title they prefer (most should prefer B), and what other titles they can think of for A (or for B!) that might be stronger. (If you wish, share our suggested alternative titles for Sample A.)

Step 4: Modeling Revision

- Share Sample C (*Whole Class Revision*) with students. Read it aloud.
- Ask students to consider the three possible titles this writer has listed, and to choose their favorite.
- Using students' suggestions, revise the draft by using a caret to insert the title they like best. If your students have a suggestion of their own that they prefer to any of the choices, by all means insert that one.

Step 5: Revising with Partners

Share Sample D (*Revising with Partners*). Read it aloud as students follow along. Then, ask students (in pairs) to follow the basic steps you modeled with Sample C. *Working with partners,* they should:

- Talk about the possible titles the writer has listed.
- Choose their favorite—OR come up with a title of their own.
- Revise by using a caret to insert the title they want (their own or one of the choices provided).
- Plan to share their choice and reasons for liking it.

Step 6: Sharing and Discussing Results

When students have finished, ask everyone to indicate with a show of hands which of the author's titles they liked best. They need not agree; there is no right answer, only reader preferences! If any pair has come up with a new title, share those aloud too, and talk about what makes each one effective.

Next Steps

- Sometimes writers forget to write a title. Is this important? Talk about it.
- Look again at any of the books you used to open this lesson. Which titles make your young readers want to hear you read the whole book? After sharing any of the books aloud, discuss whether the title was a good choice.
- As you share additional literature, continue to ask students (occasionally), "Do you think this title was a good choice? Why? Would you have chosen a different title? If so, what?"
- Invite students to help you come up with a good title for a piece you are writing.
- Encourage students to write first, and *then* come up with a title. It is much easier to think of a good title once you have the text in front of you!
- *For students who need a challenge:* Invite strong writers to read a piece of their own writing aloud to the class—without sharing the title. Let other students guess what the title might be. Then, ask the writer to share the title and the reason he or she chose it.

Sample A

A Paper on Whales

Whales may be quite small—just slightly longer than a tall man. Or, they can be almost 100 feet long and weigh more than 20 elephants! Some whales eat seals and penguins—or even other whales. Others eat tiny sea creatures called krill. Krill are like small shrimp. Though most whales are huge, many leap—or breach. If you're lucky, you might see one leap right up out of the ocean!

Sample B

Your Garden's Secret Friends

Do you like toads? You might if you have a garden. Toads eat many garden pests, including hungry beetles, caterpillars, and moths. A toad is really a kind of frog. Unlike other frogs, though, the toad lives mostly on land—not in the water. If you touch a toad, you'll find out its skin is bumpier and *drier* than a frog's. Toads might live on land, but they like water. If you turn on a sprinkler, you may coax the toads out to enjoy a shower. Maybe they'll have dinner, too!

Suggested New Titles for Sample A

____ Bigger Than 20 Elephants!

____ Amazing Whales

____ Surprising Facts About Whales

____ Gymnasts of the Ocean

Other ideas:

_____

_____

Sample C: Whole Class Revision

Butterflies can be yellow or orange—even bright blue! The butterfly starts out as an egg—which hatches into a hungry caterpillar. The caterpillar eats MANY leaves, and finally builds a little cocoon for itself, where it hangs from a branch as it *s-l-o-w-l-y* turns into a butterfly. The adult butterfly has four wings (two big, two small) and six legs. It lives for up to a year and lays two batches of eggs—which soon hatch into new little caterpillars! That starts the cycle all over again.

I could call this writing . . .

___ Beautiful Butterflies

___ From Egg to Butterfly

___ Life Cycle of the Butterfly

Or _____

Sample D: Revising with Partners

In soccer, two teams try to score goals by kicking a ball into a net. The team that scores the most goals wins. "Strikers" try to score goals. "Defenders" block shots by the other team. The "goalie" guards the net so the other team cannot score. Only the goalie can touch the ball with his or her hands. Other players use their feet (or their heads). For this reason, soccer is often called "football." Soccer is exciting because the players hardly ever stand still. In fact, soccer just might be the *most popular* sport in the world.

I could call this writing . . .

___ Soccer

___ Most Popular Sport in the World

___ A Great Game!

Or _____

Other Suggested Titles for C and D

Sample C: Whole Class Revision

___ What's Inside That Cocoon?

___ An Amazing Change

___ It Wasn't Always a Butterfly

Sample D: Revising with Partners

___ Use Your Head—or Your Feet!

___ A World Favorite

___ Another Kind of "Football"

Beginning a Sentence with a Capital

Lesson **9**

Trait Connection: **Being an Editor (Conventions)**

Introduction (Share with students in your own words)

Reading is easier when we can see where each sentence begins. If writers run their writing together, it is confusing, like this:

I love ice cream my mom makes ice cream.

This looks like one sentence. Is it, though? Read it slowly, pausing after each word. See how many sentences you hear. If you said there are two, you have a super sharp editor's ear today. Now here's the *tough* question: *Where does the first sentence end?* If you said after *ice cream* and before *my*, you are an editing star. Stand up and take a bow. Good. It's hard to tell because the writer forgot to put a period after the first sentence, or to use a capital to begin the new sentence. Capitals make sentence beginnings as easy to spot as birds in trees. (We'll worry about the periods next time.) Look at the difference:

I love ice cream. My mom makes ice cream.

There we go. That capital "M" stands out like a big flag that says, "New Sentence!" Editors often mark letters to be capitalized by writing three small lines under them, like this: <u>my</u> **mom makes ice cream.**

But you can also just write the capital over the small letter, like this: **My mom makes ice cream.**

Teaching the Lesson (General Guidelines for Teachers)

1. Show students how to mark a capital (with underscoring OR writing over).
2. Practice changing lower case letters to capitals, using our example or one of your own. Be sure to write *with your students.*
3. Share the editing lesson on the following page. Read it aloud, using inflection to indicate where sentences begin and end. Notice that the ONLY errors in this lesson are *missing capitals.* End punctuation is in place. (That comes up in the next editing lesson.)
4. Ask students to work individually first, then check with a partner. Remind them that they need to look for *3 missing capital letters.*
5. When everyone is done, ask them to *coach you* as you edit the copy on an overhead transparency.
6. When you finish, check your editing against the corrected copy.

67

Editing Practice

Put in 3 missing capitals.

Steven did NOT like shopping one bit. No, sir. why

did it always take so long? he felt very tired walking

up and down the aisles, and in and out of stores.

when his mom said it was time to go get pizza,

Steven felt like shouting for joy!

Corrected Copy

3 capitals inserted

Steven did NOT like shopping one bit. No, sir. **W**hy

did it always take so long? **H**e felt very tired walking

up and down the aisles, and in and out of stores.

When his mom said it was time to go get pizza,

Steven felt like shouting for joy!

Revising to Wrap It Up

Trait Connection: **Organization**

Introduction

Suppose a friend said to you, "So one day, there was this really HUGE thunderstorm!" [Pause.] You would be waiting for her to go on, right? If she said nothing more, you might say, "So—what's the *rest* of the story?" If she shrugged and told you, "That's *it*. That's all there is," you might say, "No, it's not! You have to tell the rest of it! You have to tell *what happened!*" We all like our stories to have endings. Endings wrap things up. They make stories—and all writing—feel finished.

Teacher's Sidebar . . .

There are many good ways to end. Telling the reader something you learned shows why your message is important. Telling the reader something you think—or *hope*—will happen lets your reader wonder and hope right along with you. Readers also love surprise endings. Reading a surprise ending is like opening an unexpected gift.

Focus and Intent

This lesson is intended to help students:

- Recognize the importance of a good ending.
- Notice the effectiveness of an ending shared aloud.
- Use what they have learned to revise a weak ending or create an ending for their own writing.

Teaching the Lesson

Step 1: Getting Writers Thinking

Endings are important. Like dessert, an ending can make or break *everything* that went before. Retrieve three or four books you have read aloud that your student writers are likely to recall—books that are favorites. With each one, ask, "Who remembers what this was about? Who remembers how it ended?" Then, read the ending—just the ending—aloud. Afterward, ask, "What makes this ending work well? What if the writer had just written THE END instead?" Does a writer even need to use THE END? (No, actually! A good ending takes the place of these words—even if movies still use them.)

Step 2: Making the Reading-Writing Connection

Here's a little game you can play with students, using any book your students *have not yet read.* My example is based on Mercer Mayer's *There's a Nightmare in My Closet,* about a young boy who can't sleep because he is frightened of the nightmare hiding in his closet. Read the whole story up to (but not including) the ending. Then, ask your students which of three possible endings is the real one:

Ending 1

So that's all I have to say about monsters. Sleep tight.

Ending 2

Well, that's the end of my story. Good night, everyone!

Ending 3

I suppose there's another nightmare in my closet, but my bed's not big enough for three.*

**Ending number 3 is Mayer's, of course. Let students vote, and then talk about why they think one ending or the other is right. If they guess correctly, reinforce this by telling them they have a good ear for endings. If not—play the game again . . . and again (using other books and endings you invent). They will get better and better (unless your made-up endings are too good, of course!).

(Mercer Mayer, *There's a Nightmare in My Closet.* 1976. New York: Puffin Books, unpaginated.)

Step 3: Involving Students as Evaluators

Ask students to look at Samples A and B as you read them aloud, paying particular attention to each ending. Have students work with a partner, and when you finish reading each one, give them a minute to talk about whether the ending works—or not.

Discussing Results

Most students should find Sample A significantly stronger. Discuss differences between A and B, asking students to tell you what they like about either ending—or what they might change. (If you wish, following your discussion, share our suggested revised endings for Sample B.)

Step 4: Modeling Revision

- Share Sample C (*Whole Class Revision*) with students. Read it aloud.
- Ask students if this ending works well. (Most should say *no.*)
- With students' help, revise the draft by adding a new ending. Cross out any or all of the old ending if you wish.

■ When you finish, read your class revision aloud. (*Optional:* Compare your revision with ours. Your copy *need not match ours.*)

Step 5: Revising with Partners

Share Sample D (*Revising with Partners*). Read it aloud as students follow along. Then, ask students (in pairs) to follow the basic steps you modeled with Sample C. *Working with partners,* they should:

■ Talk about whether the ending works.

■ Talk to each other about other ways to end the story of Max and the roller coaster.

■ Revise by changing the old ending or simply adding on to the story.

■ Read their revised endings aloud to each other.

Step 6: Sharing and Discussing Results

When students have finished, ask several pairs of students to share their revised endings aloud with the whole class. As a group, discuss the kinds of endings different teams came up with. Did some teams think of an ending no one else thought of? Good!

Next Steps

■ Remind students to *double space* their own writing.

■ Model revising an ending for a piece of your own writing. Ask students for suggestions as you revise in front of them.

■ Play "Which ending is the real one?" with other literature you share. Recommended:

- *There's a Nightmare in My Closet* by Mercer Mayer. 1976. New York: Puffin Books.

- *The Missing Mitten Mystery* by Steven Kellogg. 2000. New York: Puffin Books.

- *Surprising Sharks* by Nicola Davies. 2003. Cambridge, MA: Candlewick Press.

- *Tale of a Tadpole* by Karen Wallace. 1998. New York: DK Publishing, Inc.

■ *For students who need a challenge*: Ask students to write an original—and different—ending to any book you share aloud. Remind them that film makers often do this: They write alternate endings to the same movie, and even show them to different audiences. Books can have alternate endings, too, if we use our imaginations.

Sample A

The Best Home Ever

A stray cat moved into Kate's playhouse and slept under an old raggedy blanket. Kate discovered her one day when she heard a soft sound, like birds chirping. It was mama cat's four new yellow striped kittens! Kate knew what her mother and father would say. They would want to get rid of mama cat, kittens and all. Kate could *not* let that happen! She fed mama cat table scraps. She played her radio LOUD so no one would hear the kittens mewing. All summer, they remained her secret—until the kittens got old enough to play in the yard. "Where did THEY come from?" asked her mom, making a face. Kate was frantic. Would she lose her little friends? Her grandmother came to the rescue. "Five cats?" she said. "Now, that's just what I need in a barn full of pesky rats!" And that's how mama cat and her four little hunters found the best home ever.

Sample B

One of the Team

More than anything, Lauren wanted to be on the softball team. She could run—really fast, her brother said. She could catch a ball even with the sun in her eyes. The one thing Lauren had trouble with was batting. High balls, low balls, and right-over-the-plate balls all zipped right by her. Now she was at the tryouts, up to bat, with two strikes on her already. One more strike and she'd be out! Lauren bit her lip and gripped the bat tight, but her hands were clammy. She tried hard to watch the pitcher, waiting for the ball to fly. *Whoosh!* it came right at her. Lauren swung with all her might and hit the ball— *crack!* So now she might make the team.

One Revised Ending for Sample B

One of the Team

. . . Lauren swung with all her might and hit the ball—

crack! ~~So now she might make the team.~~

"Lauren!" the coach was yelling. "You did it! You're a

hitter! Welcome to the softball team!"

Sample C: Whole Class Revision

Mystery Package

All through the birthday party, Henry and Fuzz (whose real name was Ben) waited for Sophie to open the really BIG RED box. It was a funny shape, kind of long, with pokey sides that stuck out, and a tiny blue bow on the top that looked waaaaaay too small. Sophie took her time.

She pulled off the blue bow and tore a little hole in the side. Fuzz and Henry stood on their tiptoes to see. But they weren't tall enough. Sophie pulled more wrapping away. "What a great gift!" she said, smiling at her grandpa.

Sample D: Revising with Partners

Roller Coaster

All day, Chet and Velvet had been wondering what Max would do. Sure, it was his birthday. But would he dare ride the big roller coaster? Max handed the man his ticket. He walked up to the roller coaster. He stood there for a long time. "Are you getting on, Max?" yelled Chet. Max smiled.

Suggested Revisions of C and D

Suggested New Ending for Sample C: Whole Class Revision

Mystery Package

. . . Fuzz and Henry stood on their tiptoes to see.

But they weren't tall enough. Sophie pulled

more wrapping away. "What a great gift!" she

said, smiling at her grandpa. **She knew the**

shiny new drum set was from him.

Suggested New Ending for Sample D: Revising with Partners

Roller Coaster

. . . Max handed the man his ticket. He walked

up to the roller coaster. He stood there for a long

time. "Are you getting on, Max?" yelled Chet.

Max smiled. **Then, he jumped on board and**

buckled himself in!

Ending a Sentence with a Period

Trait Connection: **Being an Editor (Conventions)**

Introduction (Share with students in your own words)

In the last lesson, we saw how a capital letter shows where a sentence begins. A period shows where the sentence ends. It says, "Stop. That's the end of *this* thought!" If a writer forgets periods, reading can be difficult—even when new sentences begin with capitals:

My dog Hunter chases cars He could do it all day

Is there one sentence here or two? If you said there are two, you're spot on. Of course, the writer did not put in any periods, so we have to try to *imagine* them—kind of the way you imagine a pizza when you're hungry. The way an editor marks a missing period looks a little like a tiny pizza. It's a big dot with a circle around it, like this:

My dog Hunter chases cars⊙ He could do it all day⊙

OK, that's better. Now we don't have to imagine the periods—they're right there. You know why editors circle periods? It's because they're tiny. You could miss them. The circle just makes them easier to see. When you're being an *editor*, use the circle. When you are being a *writer*, you don't need the circle. Just remember to put periods in so your reader won't have to imagine them.

Teaching the Lesson (General Guidelines for Teachers)

1. Show students how to insert a period, using a dot with a circle around it.
2. Practice inserting periods, using our example or one of your own. Be sure to edit *with your students*.
3. Share the editing lesson on the following page. Read it aloud, using inflection to indicate where sentences begin and end. Notice that the ONLY errors in this lesson are *missing periods*.
4. Ask students to work individually first, then check with a partner. Remind them that they need to look for *3 missing periods*.
5. When everyone is done, ask them to *coach you* as you edit the copy on an overhead transparency.
6. When you finish, check your editing against the corrected copy.

Goal: End 3 sentences with periods. Check for missing periods in your own work.

Editing Practice

Insert 3 missing periods.

Keeping a room neat is one of the hardest

things in the world There is always one more

thing to pick up Being neat is tough

Corrected Copy

3 periods inserted

Keeping a room neat is one of the hardest

things in the world⊙ There is always one

more thing to pick up⊙ Being neat is tough⊙

Revising the Order

Trait Connection: **Organization**

Introduction

Suppose you want to make some lemonade, and you ask a friend for directions. She says, "Oh, it's easy . . . start with some lemons, only you need to *squeeze* the lemons first . . . but wait! Even before you do *that*, get out some ice, or rather, some *water* . . . no, wait! Before you do *anything* else, get out a *pitcher* . . ." Good grief. Is anybody confused yet? When it comes to directions, order is *very* important.

Teacher's Sidebar . . .

Almost no one can write out directions in order the *very first time*. Good writers begin by listing *all* the steps—without worrying about order. Then, they number them in the order they should go. That way, when they re-copy the list, they can be sure everything is in place and nothing is left out (like the sugar in our confused friend's lemonade).

Focus and Intent

This lesson is intended to help students:

- Appreciate the importance of order in directions.
- Distinguish between clear and confusing directions.
- Use what they have learned to revise the order in a set of directions.

Teaching the Lesson

Step 1: Getting Writers Thinking About Order

Warm up by listing steps for something your students do frequently, such as go to lunch, go to recess, prepare to leave for the day, and so on. Choose something everyone participates in, and something that involves several *small* steps. Ask students to brainstorm *all* the steps first, and list them *without worrying about order*. After you are done listing, number your steps. Read through them aloud to make sure everything is in order—and that you have not left anything out!

Step 2: Making the Reading-Writing Connection

In the *Frog and Toad* story called "A List," Toad makes a list of things to do during his day. He is happily following it and crossing things off—getting up, getting dressed, going for a walk with Frog—when suddenly, a strong wind snatches the list from Toad's hand:

> *"Hurry!" said Frog. "We will run and catch it."*
> *"No!" shouted Toad. "I cannot do that."*
> *"Why not?" asked Frog.*
> *"Because," wailed Toad, "running after my list is not one of the things that I wrote on my list of things to do!"*

(Arnold Lobel, "A List." In *Frog and Toad Together.* 1972. New York: HarperCollins. Unpaginated.)

Do you see poor Toad's dilemma? Is he missing the whole point of having a list? A list is supposed to make things easier for us—*but we control the list.* It doesn't control *us!* You may wish to read Lobel's whole story with your students. Use it to talk about when the *real* revision of any list occurs—*when we actually try doing the task!*

Step 3: Involving Students as Evaluators

Ask students to look at Samples A and B as you read them aloud, paying particular attention to order. Have students work with a partner, and when you finish reading each set of directions, give them a minute to talk about whether the order is helpful—or confusing. There is a space on the page to mark this with a check (✓).

Discussing Results

Most students should find Sample B significantly stronger. Discuss differences between A and B, asking students to tell you what is confusing about the tire swing directions. (If you wish, following your discussion, share our suggested revision for Sample A.)

Step 4: Modeling Revision

- Share Sample C (*Whole Class Revision*) with students. Read it aloud.
- Ask students if they think the order is helpful. (Most should say *no.*)
- With students' help, revise the draft. Add anything that was left out to the end of the list. Then, renumber the steps. You do *not* need to recopy. We want to keep this revision simple!
- When you finish, read your revised list aloud. (*Optional:* Compare your revised version with ours. Your copy *need not match ours.*)

Step 5: Revising with Partners

Share Sample D (*Revising with Partners*). Read it aloud as students follow along. Then, ask students (in pairs) to follow the basic steps you modeled with Sample C. *Working with partners,* they should:

- Talk about whether the order works.
- Add any new steps to the end of the list.
- Revise by renumbering *all* the steps.
- Read their revised list in order (aloud to each other).

Note: Students do NOT need to recopy their lists. This revision should be quick! If you wish, cut the steps into strips so students can move them around until the order seems to work—*then* number them!

Step 6: Sharing and Discussing Results

When students have finished, ask several pairs of students to share their revised lists aloud with the whole class. Did everyone come up with the same order?

Next Steps

- Remind students that when making and revising a list, it helps to get *all* the steps on paper before beginning to move things around. It also helps to cut the steps into sentence strips so you can move them—like puzzle pieces!

- Model revision of your own list. You might imagine you are going out of town for the weekend and leaving a friend some instructions for watering plants or caring for a pet. Or that you are leaving (simplified!) directions for a substitute teacher. Ask students to help you remember what's important—and put it in an order that makes sense.

- Most towns and cities print visitor maps that include visual representations of key buildings or favorite tourist spots. Such maps are ideal for practicing the writing of directions. Ask students to work in teams and provide directions for getting from one spot to another on a visual map.

- Do a critique of written directions. Recipes make great models. Recommended:
  - *Frog and Toad Together* by Arnold Lobel. 1972. New York: HarperCollins.
  - *The Everything Kids' Cookbook* by Sandra K. Nissenberg. 2002. Avon, MA: Adams Media Corporation.
  - *Fun With Kids in the Kitchen Cookbook* by Judi Rogers. 1996. Hagerstown, MD: Review & Herald Publishing.
  - *I Made It Myself* by Sandra K. Nissenberg. 1998. Minneapolis: Chronimed Publishing.
  - *The Usborne First Cookbook* by Angela Wilkes. 2007. London: Usborne Publishing.

- *For students who need a challenge:* Ask students to write an original set of directions for something in which the steps are not so obvious—such as choosing a gift for someone or making a friend. Students who like a challenge love the complexity and creativity of charting their own path.

Sample A

How to Make a Tire Swing

It is easy to make a tire swing. You need a

big rope and a tire. Then follow these steps:

1. Tie the rope to a tire.

2. Climb on!

3. Tie the rope to a strong branch.

4. Find a BIG tree for your swing.

5. Don't swing too high at first.

6. Make sure the rope is tight!

___ Clear

___ Confusing

Sample B

Setting Up the Perfect Aquarium

Want a perfect aquarium for your goldfish? Here's how

to do it:

1. Wash your fish tank and dry it.

2. Put it on a STRONG table!

3. Spread gravel over the bottom.

4. Add <u>clean</u> water.

5. Hook up a filter to <u>keep</u> the water clean.

6. Wait 5 days to add fish.

7. Add 2 fish. Then they won't be lonely!

8. Don't forget to feed your fish!

___ Clear

___ Confusing

Revised List for Sample A

How to Make a Tire Swing

It is easy to make a tire swing. You need a big rope and a tire. Then follow these steps:

___**2**___　Tie the rope to a tire.

___**5**___　Climb on!

___**3**___　Tie the rope to a strong branch.

___**1**___　Find a BIG tree for your swing.

___**6**___　Don't swing too high at first.

___**4**___　Make sure the rope is tight!

Sample C: Whole Class Revision

Planting Seeds

Have you ever planted flower seeds? Here are five steps

to make it easy!

____ Take the seeds out of the package.

____ Find a good spot to plant.

____ Put a seed in each hole.

____ Make a small hole for each seed.

____ Cover each seed with soft dirt.

Sample D: Revising with Partners

Making a Pizza

You can make your own pizza! Just follow these steps:

____ Roll out the dough.

____ Bake your pizza for 15 minutes.

____ Add some toppings.

____ Add tomato sauce.

____ Add cheese.

____ Turn on the oven.

Suggested Revisions of C and D

Sample C: Whole Class Revision

Planting Seeds

Have you ever planted flower seeds? Here are five steps
to make it easy!

3   Take the seeds out of the package.

1   Find a good spot to plant.

4   Put a seed in each hole.

2   Make a small hole for each seed.

5   Cover each seed with soft dirt.

6   Water the seeds!

Sample D: Revising with Partners

Making a Pizza

You can make your own pizza! Just follow these steps:

2   Roll out the dough.

6   Bake your pizza for 15 minutes.

5   Add some toppings.

3   Add tomato sauce.

4   Add cheese.

1   Turn on the oven.

Choosing a Period— or Question Mark

Trait Connection: **Being an Editor (Conventions)**

Introduction (Share with students in your own words)

You have had some practice inserting missing periods to show where a sentence stops. Not all sentences, though, are telling sentences that give information. Some ask questions. Which of these sentences asks a question?

- Have you seen my dog
- What time are you coming
- Who took the Ketchup

If you said "*Every single one* of them," you have a great editor's ear. How do you show a sentence is a question? If you said "Add a question mark," you are thinking like an editor. Our old friend the caret helps us do it, just like this:

- Have you seen my dog?
- What time are you coming?
- Who took the Ketchup?

Knowing whether a sentence is a telling sentence or a question makes reading easier. Telling sentences end with periods. Questions end with question marks.

Teaching the Lesson (General Guidelines for Teachers)

1. Show students how to insert a question mark, using a caret with the question mark right above it.
2. Practice inserting question marks, using our examples or your own. Be sure to edit *with your students*.
3. Remind students how to insert a period, using a circle with a dot in the middle.
4. Talk about the difference between a telling sentence (that gives information) and a question (that asks for information).
5. Share the editing lesson on the following page. Read it aloud, using inflection to help students hear which sentences are telling sentences and which one is a question. The ONLY errors in this lesson are *missing end punctuation*.
6. Ask students to work individually first, then check with a partner.
7. When everyone is done, ask them to *coach you* as you edit the copy on an overhead transparency.
8. When you finish, check your editing against the corrected copy.

Goal: Insert missing periods or question marks in 3 sentences.
Check your own sentences to see which need periods and which need question marks.

Editing Practice

Edit 3 sentences so they end with a period or question mark.

Almost everyone loves hot dogs Do you like

them done in a pan or on the grill If you ask

me, hot dogs on the grill are the best

Corrected Copy

3 periods or question marks inserted

Almost everyone loves hot dogs⊙ Do you like

them done in a pan or on the grill? If you ask

me, hot dogs on the grill are the best⊙

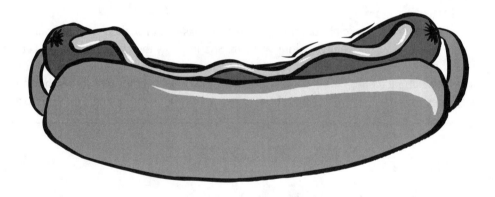

Revising with Feelings

Lesson 14

Trait Connection: **Voice**

Introduction

Voice is mostly about feelings. When your best friend is angry or worried, you just *know*, don't you? You don't need your friend to hold up a sign saying, "I'm mad today" or "I feel nervous." You can tell from the look on your friend's face—or from how he or she acts. Good writing is like that. Good writing lets us tell a lot about someone's feelings from what they say or how they act—or (when the book has pictures) from the looks on their faces. Sometimes—did you ever notice this?—even the colors inside a book show something about people's feelings.

Teacher's Sidebar . . .
Some people like to write about *other* people's feelings—but not their own. If your students feel like that, it's OK. Their feelings belong to *them*. Sharing how they feel is a choice. Let them know that when they write about feeling disappointed, or excited, or hurt, or jealous, or nervous, they are writing about feelings their readers have had, too. It helps readers to know they are not the only ones who have strong feelings about things. In sharing their feelings, they share their voice.

Focus and Intent

This lesson is intended to help students:

- Connect feelings to the trait of voice.
- Distinguish between writing that has voice and writing that is without voice.
- Revise a piece by showing a character's feelings.

Teaching the Lesson

Step 1: Getting Writers Thinking About Feelings

Warm up by talking about the different kinds of feelings people have. They can feel frightened, nervous, surprised, excited, hopeful, jealous, hurt, disappointed, sad, and so on. Ask students to model facial expressions that might go with various feelings. Then, ask them to act out some of the actions that might go with a particular feeling. For example, how does an excited person walk—or talk—or eat? What about a sad person? An angry person? . . . and so on.

Step 2: Making the Reading-Writing Connection

Sophie is the main character in Molly Bang's book *When Sophie Gets Angry—Really, Really Angry*. When the story begins, Sophie is having a hard time sharing Gorilla (a favorite toy) with her sister. (Ask students if they have had this experience.) Things dissolve into a tussle, and Sophie loses her composure (if you have the book, share the page showing her face):

> *She kicks. She screams. She wants to smash the world to smithereens. She roars a red, red roar.*
>
> (Molly Bang, *When Sophie Gets Angry—Really, Really Angry*. 1999. New York: Scholastic. Unpaginated.)

Why would Sophie roar "a red, red roar"? What do your students think about Molly Bang's choice of color to show how Sophie feels? Would a "blue, blue roar" or a "gray, gray roar" work the same way? You may wish to read the whole story with your students. If you do, ask them to notice how the color changes as the story continues. What happens? What do colors show about Sophie's feelings? How do both change through the book?

Step 3: Involving Students as Evaluators

Ask students to look at Samples A and B as you read them aloud, paying particular attention to voice (expressed through feelings). Have students work with a partner, and when you finish reading each sample, give them a minute to talk about how much voice the piece has. There is a line running from **No Voice** to **Max Voice** where they can mark with an **x.**

Discussing Results

Most students should find Sample A significantly stronger. Discuss differences between A and B, asking students to tell you what parts of A show voice, or what they wish the writer in Sample B would do to show *more* voice. (If you wish, share our suggested revision for Sample B.)

Step 4: Modeling Revision

- Share Sample C (*Whole Class Revision*) with students. Read it aloud.
- Ask students if they think the voice is strong. (Most should say *no*.)
- Talk about how Kyle is feeling, and what he might do (or say) to show those feelings. Then, with students' help, revise the draft.
- When you finish, read your revision aloud. (*Optional:* Compare your revision with ours. Your copy *need not match ours*.)

Step 5: Revising with Partners

Share Sample D (*Revising with Partners*). Read it aloud as students follow along. Then, ask students (in pairs) to follow the basic steps you modeled with Sample C. *Working with partners,* they should:

- Talk about whether the voice is strong.
- Talk about Dagen's feelings—and what she might do to show her feelings.
- Revise by adding details that show how Dagen feels.
- Read their revision aloud to each other.

Step 6: Sharing and Discussing Results

When students have finished, ask several pairs of students to share their revisions aloud with the whole class. Did people come up with different details? Are there many different kinds of actions that can show feelings?

Next Steps

- Remind students to *double space* their writing—in case they want to add details.

- Model revision with voice by changing a piece of your own writing to show your own feelings more honestly. Examples might be a thank you note to a friend, or a review of a film or book that you put online. Begin with a fairly flat version—then let students coach you as you put more feeling into the piece.

- Share other literature in which feelings play a key role, asking students to note how the characters *look, speak, and act,* and how that helps us understand their feelings. Recommended:

  - *When Sophie Gets Angry—Really, Really Angry* by Molly Bang. 1999. New York: Scholastic.
  - *Koala Lou* by Mem Fox. 1994. New York: Voyager Books.
  - *Parts* by Tedd Arnold. 1997. New York: Puffin Books.
  - *What You Know First* by Patricia MacLachlan. 1995. New York: HarperCollins.

- Art plays a key role in expressing voice. When students write about feelings—their own or someone else's—encourage them to create art to go with the text, and to use color to express mood.

- *For students who need a challenge*: Using Molly Bang's book as a model, ask students to write an original narrative in which the central character (animal or person—can be the writer) changes from one mood or feeling to another. The character might go from glum to excited, for example—or nervous to relaxed. Encourage writers to create art that reflects the change.

Sample A

Fast Food

Regie Rat scurried down the alleyway behind the old restaurant, sniffing for crumbs. There was *nothing!* Not one measly bite of doughnut. "Rats!" he muttered. He wrinkled his nose and let his tiny shoulders droop. Just then—footsteps!

Regie ducked into the shadows as a woman wolfing down a HUGE burger stepped into the alley. Regie's pink eyes widened. He drooled as Ketchup slid off the burger and splashed onto the street. A small piece of meat wriggled loose and hung on by a thread. "Come on . . . come *ON* . . ." Regie whispered, eyeing it closely. And then—the meat dropped.

In one furry flash, Regie dashed between the woman's feet, snatched the morsel in his long teeth, and dove for cover. He swallowed the meat in one gulp, licking juice from his scruffy chin. A ratty yellow-toothed smile spread over his face.

No Voice   Max Voice

Sample B

A Special Cake

Erika worked all day on a cake for her grandfather's

birthday. It was the first thing she had ever baked herself.

Erika's mom asked if she wanted help, but Erika said no. She

wanted to do *everything* herself.

She put all the ingredients together in a big bowl, stirred it

well, and poured the batter into a cake pan the shape of a heart.

Carefully, she lifted the cake pan into the hot oven, shut the door,

and set the timer. Then she went out to the porch to read.

Later, she went back to get her cake from the oven. She

was surprised. The cake had burned. Erika felt bad.

No Voice   **Max Voice**

_____

Suggested Revision for Sample B

A Special Cake

Erika worked all day on a cake for her grandfather's

birthday. It was the first thing she had ever baked herself.

Erika's mom asked if she wanted help, but Erika said no. She

wanted to do *everything* herself.

She put all the ingredients together in a big bowl, stirred it

well, and poured the batter into a cake pan the shape of a heart.

She smiled because the heart showed how she felt about her grandpa.
Carefully, she lifted the cake pan into the hot oven, shut the door,
humming to herself,
and set the timer. Then, she went out to the porch to read.

Later, she went back to get her cake from the oven. ~~She~~

~~was surprised. The cake had burned. Erika felt bad,~~ **She could**

not believe her eyes! Smoke was coming from her cake—it

looked like charcoal. Tears filled Erika's eyes and her

heart felt as heavy as a rock.

Sample C: Whole Class Revision

First-Time Driver

Kyle was helping his grandmother in the pumpkin patch when a storm came up. "Hop in the truck," Grandma said. "We'll race the storm back to the house and get inside!"

As she pulled herself in, Grandma made a face. She had twisted her right ankle—badly. "You'll have to drive," she told Kyle. She handed him the keys. "Don't worry—it's just down the old gravel road."

Kyle had never driven in his whole life. He was worried.

Sample D: Revising with Partners

No Fair!

Dagen wanted to go to the movies. Mom said she could go if she took her little sister, Rae. On the way, Rae decided she wanted to go home. She began to cry—*very* loudly.

"Shhhh," Dagen told her, "You'll *love* the movies! I'll buy you popcorn!" But Rae would not stop screaming. Finally, they just had to go home.

Dagen was not happy.

Suggested Revisions of C and D

Sample C: Whole Class Revision

First-Time Driver

. . . "You'll have to drive," she told Kyle. She handed him the keys. "Don't worry—it's just down the old gravel road."

Kyle had never driven in his whole life. ~~He was worried.~~ His hands were shaking. He felt very small behind the big wheel of the truck.

Sample D: Revising with Partners

No Fair!

. . . But Rae would not stop screaming. Finally, they just had to go home.

~~Dagen was not happy.~~ Dagen stomped along the sidewalk. She did not smile or talk to Rae. She did not say one single word the whole way home.

Choosing a Period— or Exclamation Point

Trait Connection: **Being an Editor (Conventions)**

Introduction (Share with students in your own words)

You have inserted missing periods and question marks. Sometimes, a writer likes to use a third mark, an exclamation point, to show strong feelings. Think about these sentences. Which ones could use exclamation points?

1. Your hat is on fire

2. Please pass the salt

3. Here comes a shark

4. I think I'll watch TV

If you said "Sentence 1 and Sentence 3," you are making good editorial choices. If you put exclamation points after ALL these sentences, you would sound like a person WHO IS VERY EXCITED ALL THE TIME!!! Let's calm down and do some editing. Remember how to put in a period? Dot and circle—right on. The caret can help us put in an exclamation point, just as it helped us with question marks:

1. Your hat is on fire!

2. Please pass the salt.

3. Here comes a shark!

4. I think I'll watch TV.

Teaching the Lesson (General Guidelines for Teachers)

1. Show students how to insert an exclamation point, using a caret with the exclamation point right above it.

2. Practice inserting exclamation points, using our examples or your own. Be sure to edit *with your students*.

3. Remind students how to insert a period, using a circle with a period right in the middle.

4. Explain that exclamation points are never *required*—but they work well when a writer wants to show excitement. It's best not to use TOO many.

5. Share the editing lesson on the following page. Read it aloud, using inflection to help students hear which sentence *might* call for an exclamation point. The ONLY errors in this lesson are *missing end punctuation.*

6. Ask students to work individually first, then check with a partner. Remind them that they need to insert a period or exclamation point at the end of each sentence. They must decide which one to use.

7. When everyone is done, ask them to *coach you* as you edit the copy on an overhead transparency.

8. When you finish, check your editing against the corrected copy.

Goal: Choose a period or exclamation point for 3 sentences.
Choose between periods and exclamation points in your own writing.

Editing Practice

Choose a period or exclamation point to end 3 sentences.

Ben and Izzie were hiking along a river

Suddenly, Izzie's foot slipped and she fell

10 feet down the rocky cliff She was not

hurt, though

Corrected Copy

Periods and exclamation points inserted*

Ben and Izzie were hiking along a river⊙

Suddenly, Izzie's foot slipped and she fell

10 feet down the rocky cliff﹗ She was not

hurt, though⊙

---

*Note
It is important to put some kind of punctuation at the end of each sentence.
A student editor is not required to use any exclamation points, however—
and he or she could use more than one. This is an editor's choice—but it
is important to notice that the second sentence is the most dramatic.

Revising with SFX (Special Effects)

Trait Connection: **Voice**

Introduction

It's easier to write with voice if we practice *reading* with voice. That means reading with expression, hitting some words harder than others, like a drum beat. For example, suppose you had a little brother who kept running in and out of your room when you were trying to do something important. You might say, "Please shut the door." What if he didn't, though? Then, maybe you'd say, "*Please* shut the door!" Try it. [Pause for student response.] What if he still didn't listen? How would you say it the third time? [Pause for student response.] Did you hit the word "door" pretty hard that time? If we wrote out the words just the way you said them, they might look like this: "PLEASE shut the DOOR!!!!" [Print this out.] If you saw that in a book, you'd know the speaker was pretty upset.

Teacher's Sidebar . . .

Many special effects can tell a reader, "Read this with *expression!*" A writer can use FULL CAPS (meaning all capital letters) to say, "Shout this out!" Sometimes writers underline* words or put in extra question marks or exclamation points. Watch for these special effects as you read.

*Underlining and using *italics* are really just two different ways of doing the same thing. You can decide if you wish to teach this to students, or just use underlining.

Focus and Intent

This lesson is intended to help students:

- Understand that conventional "special effects" change the way we read print.
- Recognize special effects (FULL CAPS or extra question marks and exclamation points) that call for reading the text with expression.
- Revise a piece to include one or more special effects.

Teaching the Lesson

Step 1: Getting Writers Thinking About SFX (Special Effects)

Warm up by asking students to listen for the emphasis in oral language. Read a sample sentence or two, asking them to listen and tell you which word(s) you hit hardest. Where is the drum beat? (You may wish to write these sentences out for students to see):

- I have the BEST cat in the WORLD.
- No one can run faster than my sister.
- Who took the LAST POPSICLE???!!!

Ask students to practice reading these aloud with you.

Step 2: Making the Reading-Writing Connection

Author Kate Lum uses plenty of special effects in *WHAT! CRIED GRANNY: An Almost Bedtime Story*. Patrick is having his first sleep-over at Granny's house, where he discovers, little by little, that Granny is missing a few things he needs—a bed, blanket, teddy bear, and pillow. Not to worry. Granny to the rescue:

> *"But Granny," said Patrick . . . "I don't HAVE a pillow here!"*
> *"WHAT?!?" cried Granny.*
> *She ran out to her henhouse, woke up the chickens, and collected a big batch of feathers.*
> *She took them to her sewing room where she made a bag of cloth. Then she stuffed it with the feathers, sewed it up neatly, and gave it to Patrick.*

(Kate Lum. *WHAT! CRIED GRANNY: An Almost Bedtime Story*. 1998. New York: Puffin Books. Unpaginated.)

You can show this small sample to students by writing out what Patrick and Granny *say*—or better yet, read the whole book, and ask students to look for FULL CAPS or extra question marks and exclamation points. Talk about how these special effects help the reader know just where the beats fall!

Step 3: Involving Students as Evaluators

Ask students to look at Samples A and B as you read them aloud, paying particular attention to voice (expressed through special effects). Have students work with a partner, and when you finish reading each sample, give them a minute to talk about whether the writer makes use of special effects—or *could*.

Discussing Results

Most students should notice special effects in Sample A. Ask students to tell you what these special effects tell a reader about reading the text aloud. Ask where or how they might use special effects for Sample B. (If you wish, share our suggested revision for Sample B.)

Step 4: Modeling Revision

- Share Sample C (*Whole Class Revision*) with students. Read it aloud.
- Ask students to listen for where the beats fall as you read.
- Ask them to help you put in any special effects that could show a reader how to read Sample C aloud with expression.

- To create FULL CAPS, simply cross out the text and print the words in FULL CAPS right above.

- When you finish, read your revision aloud with plenty of emphasis! (*Optional:* Compare your revision with ours. Your copy *need not match ours.* Special effects are not required, but they are fun!)

Step 5: Revising with Partners

Share Sample D (*Revising with Partners*). Read it aloud as students follow along. You may wish to do this more than once. Then, ask students (in pairs) to follow the basic steps you modeled with Sample C. *Working with partners,* they should:

- Talk about where the beats fall.
- Talk about what kinds of special effects—underlining, FULL CAPS, or extra exclamation points or question marks—could add emphasis.
- Revise by adding one or more special effects.
- Read their revision aloud to each other—with plenty of voice!

Step 6: Sharing and Discussing Results

When students have finished, ask several pairs of students to share their revisions aloud with the whole class. Did everyone hear the "beat" in the same spot? Probably not!

Next Steps

- Remind students to *double space* their writing—in case they want to add special effects such as FULL CAPS.

- Revise a piece of your own writing by adding special effects. Be careful not to *overdo* it. Special effects are a <u>LOT</u> of *fun, but* if we put them *everywhere,* THEY <u>LOSE</u> THEIR SPECIALNESS!!!! DON'T YOU <u>THINK</u>????? *WOW!!!!!!!!!!*

- Share other literature that makes effective use of special effects. Recommended:
  - *WHAT! CRIED GRANNY: An Almost Bedtime Story* by Kate Lum. 1998. New York: Puffin Books.
  - *Don't Let the Pigeon Stay Up Late* by Mo Willems. 2006. New York: Hyperion Books for Children.
  - *I Am Too Absolutely Small for School* by Lauren Child. 2003. Cambridge, MA: Candlewick Press.

- *For students who need a challenge:* This lesson explores only a few of the many conventional special effects that can be used to create and emphasize voice. Ask students who are ready for a challenge to explore other literature to see what they can find—e.g., tiny print, **boldface** print, *italics*, ellipses (. . . for a pause to think), different fonts, repeated letters: *pleeeeeeeeeeease!!!* . . . and so on. If they have computer access, they can put some of these special effects to work, or build a **SFX Collection**!!!

Sample A

Not in MY Lunch!!!!

Lucy's brother Flip was making her lunch for school.

Lucy was NOT in the mood for something different.

"Just TRY it, Lucy!" said Flip.

"Not in a MILLION YEARS!!!" she answered.

"One olive won't <u>kill</u> you, you know," Flip told her.

"It <u>could</u>," Lucy replied. "You don't know how

powerful olives can be."

Flip sighed. "Your lunch is SO boring!!!!!" he said,

closing the bag.

"Well, not to <u>me</u>," said Lucy. "And <u>I'm</u> the one eating it."

Sample B

A Big Deal

Jack did not want help blowing out his birthday candles. "It's my cake," he said. "I want to blow out my own candles."

"I just want to help," squealed his sister Sara.

"No," said Jack. "You are not helping and that's final."

Uncle Fred figured out what to do. Jack blew out the candles. Sara got to take a picture.

Suggested Revision of Sample B

A Big Deal

Jack did ~~not~~ ^{NOT} want help blowing out his birthday

candles. "It's ~~my~~ ^{MY} cake," he said. "I want to blow out my

own candles."

"I just want to help," squealed his sister Sara.

"NO!!!!"

~~"No,"~~ said Jack. "You are not helping and that's final."

Uncle Fred figured out what to do. Jack blew out the

candles. Sara got to take a picture.

Sample C: Whole Class Revision

Stop, Thief!

Who was taking Brad's socks? The pile in his drawer got smaller by the day.

One morning, he spotted Goldie, his yellow Lab. Goldie was tugging socks out of the laundry basket. "Stop that," yelled Brad.

Goldie did not stop. In fact, she grabbed three more socks. "No," Brad yelled. As he leaped for her, Goldie shot out the door. Brad was left with one sock.

Sample D: Revising with Partners

Growing to the Sky

Ms. Miller's second grade class planted sunflower seeds.

They watered them every day. They grew and grew.

Soon, they were pretty big. Then, they got really big.

Then, they got huge.

"Good grief," said one of the kids. "I think we can climb

these things."

Suggested Revisions of C and D

Sample C: Whole Class Revision

Stop, Thief!

Who was taking Brad's socks? **???** The pile in his drawer got smaller by the day.

One morning, he spotted Goldie, his yellow Lab. Goldie was tugging socks out of the laundry basket. "Stop that **!**" yelled Brad.

Goldie did ~~not~~ **NOT** stop. In fact, she grabbed three more socks. "~~No~~" **"NO!!!"** Brad yelled. As he leaped for her, Goldie shot out the door. Brad was left with ~~one~~ **ONE** sock.

Sample D: Revising with Partners

Growing to the Sky

Ms. Miller's second grade class planted sunflower seeds.

They watered them every day. They grew and grew.

Soon, they were pretty big. Then, they got really big. Then, they got ~~huge~~ **HUGE!!!**

"Good grief," said one of the kids. "I think we can ~~climb~~ **CLIMB** these things **!**"

Putting It Together
(Lessons 9, 11, 13, and 15)

Trait Connection: **Being an Editor (Conventions)**

Introduction (Share with students in your own words)

You've had some practice showing how sentences begin and end. As an editor, you know a sentence needs to begin with a capital letter. You also know sentences can end in different ways. Think about these three sentences. Which one would end with a period, which with a question mark, and which with an exclamation point?

1. there's a spider on your sandwich
2. who ate the last cookie
3. i picked some flowers

If you put an exclamation point after sentence 1, a question mark after 2, and a period after 3, your editor's radar is really working today. Wait, though—do you remember how to add all those marks? Circle and dot for a period—and carets for the other two. To change a lower case to a capital, write the capital right over the top, just like this:

1. **T**here's a spider on your sandwich**!**
2. **W**ho ate the last cookie**?**
3. **I** picked some flowers**⊙**

Teaching the Lesson (General Guidelines for Teachers)

1. Remind students how to change lower case letters to capitals, and how to insert periods, question marks, or exclamation points.
2. Practice using these marks—with our examples or ones you make up. Be sure to edit *with students so they can see just how it is done and copy you.*
3. Share the editing lesson on the following page. Read it aloud with expression so it is easy for students to hear where sentences end, and which one is a question. Notice that there are *no capitals* to begin sentences, and *no end punctuation.* Student editors must figure out where sentences start and stop.
4. Ask students to work individually first, then check with a partner. Remind them to look and listen for *three sentences.* Each one should begin with a capital letter and end with a period, question mark, or exclamation point.
5. When everyone is done, ask them to *coach you* as you edit the copy on an overhead transparency.
6. When you finish, check your editing against the corrected copy.

Goal: Insert capitals and end punctuation for 3 sentences. Make sure sentences in your own writing begin with a capital and end with the right punctuation.

Editing Practice

Edit 3 sentences.

what a beautiful day it was the sun was

shining brightly would Andy and his dad

catch a fish

Corrected Copy

3 sentences edited

What a beautiful day it was! The sun was

shining brightly. Would Andy and his dad

catch a fish?

Note
It is all right to substitute a period for the exclamation point after the
first sentence. Exclamation points show expression—but are optional.
What is most important is for the student to know where each sentence
begins and ends—and to recognize the one sentence that is a question.

Revising with "Wake-Up" Details

Trait Connection: **Voice**

Introduction

Writers who know their topics well find it *easy* to write with voice. That's because they always seem to have an unusual detail to share with the reader—the way you share a special secret with a friend. Exciting or unusual details wake readers right up. After all, readers don't want to miss out on any secrets!

Teacher's Sidebar . . .

A "wake-up" detail can be absolutely *anything* that is interesting—and that the reader might not know already. Readers know, for instance, that elephants are big—or that ants can spoil picnics. But maybe some readers do *not* know that elephants can live to be 65 years old, or that some kinds of ants can store so much honey in their bodies that they swell up like tiny grapes. Every time good writers learn something new, they tuck it away in their "mental notebooks." Who knows? They might want to write about it sometime—and put more voice into their writing.

Focus and Intent

This lesson is intended to help students:

- Understand that interesting or unusual information enhances voice.
- Recognize "wake-up" details in writing they read or hear.
- Revise a piece by choosing the most unusual bit of information from several possibilities.

Teaching the Lesson

Step 1: Getting Writers Thinking About Wake-Up Details

Warm up by asking students to think about the things that make your classroom, school, or city/town (choose ONE to focus on) different from others. During your discussion, make two lists: **Things Most People Know** and **Things Most People DON'T Know**. See how big you can make the second list. Feel free to add your own details, always making sure to ask students, "Do you think most people would know this?" Finally, ask students to identify the two or three most interesting things the whole group came up with. "When you write," tell them, "you want to include 'wake-up' details like these!"

Step 2: Making the Reading-Writing Connection

Author Dick King-Smith used to be a dairy farmer—and is now a full-time author. As anyone who's read *Babe: The Gallant Pig* can tell you, Dick King-Smith loves pigs. In the book *All Pigs Are Beautiful*, he compares pigs to people, and it seems we have a lot in common. Maybe some things in this passage about mother pigs—called *sows*—won't surprise you. But there's *one* pretty surprising fact. Which one is it? Does it add to the voice?

> *Sows spend their lives having babies, lots of them, and they take as good care of them as your mom does of you. Well, almost. Trouble is, newborn piglets are so small that sometimes the sow lies down and squashes one. Your mother would never do that to you—I hope!*

(Dick King-Smith. *All Pigs Are Beautiful.* 1993. Cambridge, MA: Candlewick Press. Unpaginated.)

Many people know pigs have lots of babies—and even that pigs make good mothers. But did you know they sometimes lie down on top of their own children? Goodness. That's enough to wake *anyone* up.

Step 3: Involving Students as Evaluators

Ask students to look at Samples A and B as you read them aloud, listening for "wake-up" details. Have students work with a partner, and when you finish reading each sample, give them a minute to talk about whether the writer incorporated any "wake-up" details—or mostly included things readers already knew.

Discussing Results

Students will likely notice several wake-up details in Sample B—but not in A. Ask students to tell you what these special details are and talk about whether they add voice (excitement). Ask if anyone knows a wake-up detail that could be added to Sample A. (If you wish, share our suggested wake-up details and revision for Sample A.)

Step 4: Modeling Revision

- Share Sample C (*Whole Class Revision*) with students. Read it aloud.
- Share the list of three details—and ask students which one makes the best "wake-up" detail. (We have chosen a favorite, but there is no "right" answer. They should choose the one *they* think is most interesting—or insert one of their own.)
- Revise by adding that wake-up detail *anywhere* in the text that it seems to fit. (You do not need to match our suggestion.)
- When you finish, read your revision aloud and listen for voice. Did adding that extra little something make a difference? (*Optional:* Compare your revision with ours. Your copy *need not match ours.*)

Step 5: Revising with Partners

Share Sample D (*Revising with Partners*). Read it aloud as students follow along. Also read the list of new details aloud. Then, ask students (in pairs) to follow the basic steps you modeled with Sample C. *Working with partners,* they should:

- Talk about whether the sample includes any "wake-up" details yet.

- Look at the list of new details, and choose the ONE they think would be most interesting to readers.

- Revise by adding that detail *anywhere* in the text that it seems to fit (or by adding a wake-up detail of their own).

- Read their revision aloud to each other—with plenty of voice!

Step 6: Sharing and Discussing Results

When students have finished, ask several pairs of students to share their revisions aloud with the whole class. Did everyone add the same "wake-up" detail?

Next Steps

- Remind students to *double space* their writing—in case they ever need to add a wake-up detail.

- Revise a piece of your own writing by adding a wake-up detail. In modeling, you might wish to share two or three possibilities, and ask students to help you choose the one they think is most interesting.

- Continue to look and listen for wake-up details in the literature you share aloud. Recommended:
  - *All Pigs Are Beautiful* by Dick King-Smith. 1993. Cambridge, MA: Candlewick Press.
  - *Animals Nobody Loves* by Seymour Simon. 2001. New York: Random House.
  - *Surprising Sharks* by Nicola Davies. 2003. Cambridge, MA: Candlewick Press.
  - *Tale of a Tadpole* by Karen Wallace. 1998. New York: DK Publishing.
  - *Tigress* by Dick Dowson. 2004. Cambridge, MA: Candlewick Press.

- *For students who need a challenge:* In this lesson, students are given additional information from which to work—and this is a good way to begin instruction in researching techniques. Some students may be ready for the next step, which is to dig up their own "wake-up details," from the Internet, or from first-hand experience (a visit to a museum or zoo, for example), or even from an interview. Provide some coaching on where and how, and then see what details they can uncover. Ask them to share both the details and their research methods with the rest of the class.

Sample A

Bats

Bats are not birds, but they have wings. They

can fly. Bats eat things like insects or mice.

They can fly at night. That is when they look

for food.

Wake-Up Details?

___ Yes!   ___ No

Sample B

Sharks

Sharks live in salt water. They are born knowing how to hunt. They have eyes on the sides of their heads—like horses. They can see behind them as well as in front. Sharks can be huge, as long as a small bus. Or, they can be about the length of a pencil! People are terrified of sharks, but the truth is, dogs and horses kill more people every year than sharks do!

Wake-Up Details?

___ Yes!   ___ No

Suggested "Wake-Up" Details for Sample A

Bats

Choose the *most interesting* one:

___ 1. Bats do not get caught in people's hair.

___ 2. Bats cry out, and the echo from their call helps them

find their way in the dark.

___ 3. Some eat fruit.

If you chose detail #2, your revision might look like this:

Bats

Bats are not birds, but they have wings. They can fly. Bats eat things like insects or mice. They can fly at night. **Bats cry out, and the echo from their call helps them find their way in the dark.** That is when they look for food.

> **Question . . .**
> Could you add *more than one* wake-up detail?
> (Sure!)

Sample C: Whole Class Revision

Amazing Spiders

Spiders live everywhere. Chances are, there is a spider near you right now! All spiders spin silk. Some use silk to make "ropes" to swing from or "balloons" to float on. They also make webs in which to trap their favorite food: insects!

Choose a "wake-up" detail to add:

1. Spiders have eight legs.

2. Some spiders bite, but most are not poisonous.

3. If spiders didn't eat them, insects would take over the world!

Sample D: Revising with Partners

The Powerful Grizzly

You could go your whole life without seeing a grizzly bear—except in the movies. There are only a few hundred left. If you do see one, it can be thrilling, but also scary. A grizzly is strong enough to kill an elk for dinner. It is best to stay far back and not bother it.

Choose a "wake-up" detail to add:

1. Grizzlies are big and strong.

2. A grizzly can stand up on its hind legs.

3. A grizzly's claws are as long as your little finger.

Suggested Revisions of C and D

Sample C: Whole Class Revision

Amazing Spiders

Spiders live everywhere. Chances are, there is a spider near you right now! All spiders spin silk. Some use silk to make "ropes" to swing from or "balloons" to float on. They also make webs in which to trap their favorite food: insects! **If spiders didn't eat them, insects would take over the world!**

Sample D: Revising th Partners

The Powerful Grizzly

You could go your whole life without seeing a grizzly bear— except in the movies. There are only a few hundred left. If you do see one, it can be thrilling, but also scary. A grizzly is strong enough to kill an elk for dinner. **A grizzly's claws are as long as your little finger.** It is best to stay far back and not bother it.

On the Lookout: What, When, Where

Trait Connection: **Being an Editor (Conventions)**

Introduction (Share with students in your own words)

It's the funniest thing. Little words can sometimes be the trickiest ones to spell right! Let's say a person writes, "What time is the concert?" Which word do you think the person is likely to spell wrong? If you said *concert*, that's a GREAT guess. But the truth is, many people will spell *concert* correctly—but get the word *what* wrong. How crazy is *that?* Too often, writers don't pay enough attention to the little words. Readers do, though! Spelling little words wrong can leave readers confused. It pays to take our time.

Let's see how you do as an editor on the lookout. Editors who are on the lookout are watching for sneaky little misspelled words so they can find them before picky readers do. If you find *what, when,* or *where* misspelled, cross out the misspelled word and use a caret to put the correct word in the line right above, like this:

What
- ~~Wat~~ time is it?

When
- ~~Wen~~ will we go?

Where
- ~~Were~~ is my book?

Teaching the Lesson (General Guidelines for Teachers)

1. Show students how to correct spelling by crossing out the misspelled words, and using a caret (^) to insert the correctly spelled word in the line above.

2. Practice correcting misspelled words, using our examples or your own. Be sure to edit *with your students, asking for their spelling help as you work.*

3. Remind students that they will have correct versions of *what, when,* and *where* to look at as they edit.

4. Share the editing lesson on page 130. Read it aloud, pronouncing misspelled words correctly. The ONLY errors in this lesson are misspelled versions of *what, when,* and *where,* one of each.

5. Ask students to work individually first, then check with a partner. Remind them to look at the correctly spelled words at the top of the page to check their spelling.

6. When everyone is done, ask them to *coach you* as you edit the copy on an overhead transparency.

7. When you finish, check your editing against the corrected copy.

Goal: Correct 3 misspelled words: *what, when, where*
Be on the lookout for <u>little</u> misspelled words in your own work.

Editing Practice

Correcting spelling:
- **what**
- **when**
- **where**

Wen his cat ran away, Ira did not know wat

to do. Were in the world <u>was</u> she??? Ira

didn't know!

Corrected Copy

Corrected spelling:
- **what**
- **when**
- **where**

When
~~Wen~~ his cat ran away, Ira did not know ~~wat~~ what

Where
to do. ~~Were~~ in the world <u>was</u> she??? Ira

didn't know!

Revising "Nice" to Add Spice

Trait Connection: **Word Choice**

Introduction

What's your very favorite food? Pizza? Burgers? Fried chicken? No matter how much you love it, you probably wouldn't want to eat it *every single day of your life!* Words can be like that. One word that's used a lot is *nice*. People are always saying, "I had a *nice* time," or "It's a *nice* day." *Nice* is a handy word. But sometimes you might wonder, "Isn't there *another* way to say it?" Instead of saying it's a *nice* day, we could say it's a *beautiful, magnificent, delightful, sun-shiny, unbelievable,* or downright *glorious* day. New or different words add spice to writing the way new and different food adds spice to lunch or dinner.

Teacher's Sidebar . . .

There is nothing wrong with the word *nice*. And there is no need to ban the word from your students' vocabulary! The trick—as with pizza—is to not overdo it. Finding alternatives gives writers options, and options always make for stronger writing.

Focus and Intent

This lesson is intended to help students:

- Understand that usually, there are many ways to say something.
- Think of alternatives for the overused word *nice*.
- Revise a piece by thinking of new ways to express an idea.

Teaching the Lesson

Step 1: Getting Writers Thinking About Options

Warm up by asking students to brainstorm some alternatives for the word *nice*. Think of as many as you can (you can add to the list, too), and write them down—in BIG print! That way, your students can use this same list later when they do some revision on Samples C and D. Having options to look at is very helpful, and makes it less likely students will avoid a word because they are not sure of the spelling. You want to encourage them to s-t-r-e-t-c-h for new ways to say things, even if they're not sure how to spell a word yet.

Step 2: Making the Reading-Writing Connection

In the book *All Pigs Are Beautiful*, author Dick King-Smith writes:

> *If you really twisted my arm and said, "You have to have a favorite kind of pig. What is it?" then I might have to say, "A black-and-white spotted, medium-snouted, flop-eared pig that comes from Gloucester"* . . .

(Dick King-Smith. *All Pigs Are Beautiful*. 1993. Cambridge, MA: Candlewick Press. Unpaginated.)

You probably know what a black-and-white pig might look like. But what about "medium-snouted"? If you know that the pig's snout is his nose, does that help you picture a "medium-snouted" pig? Let's think about "flop-eared" for a minute. What do you suppose that might look like? You could try imitating it with your hands. If you pictured ears drooping forward, you'd be right. If Dick King-Smith had just written "I like pigs—they're nice," we wouldn't have these terrific pictures in our heads.

Step 3: Involving Students as Evaluators

Ask students to look at Samples A and B as you read them aloud, listening for the word *nice*—and asking if one writer uses it a little too much. (At the bottom of each sample is a place to check "yes" or "no.") When you finish reading each sample, give students a minute to talk with a partner about whether there might be another way to say how "nice" something is.

Discussing Results

Students will likely notice that the word *nice* is used several times in Sample A—but not in B. Ask if anyone can think of another way to express some of the ideas in Sample A. Remind students that *nice* is a perfectly good word—now and then! We just don't want to make it the *only* word we use to say we like or admire something. (If you wish, share our suggested revision for Sample A.)

Step 4: Modeling Revision

- Share Sample C (*Whole Class Revision*) with students. Read it aloud.
- Ask students if they think the word *nice* is used too many times. (Most should say *yes*.)
- Ask students for suggestions on "other ways to say it."
- Revise by replacing *nice* one or more times with a different word or expression.
- When you finish, read your revision aloud. Did replacing *nice* add a little spice to your writing? (*Optional:* Compare your revision with ours. Your copy *need not match ours*.)

133

Step 5: Revising with Partners

Share Sample D (*Revising with Partners*). Read it aloud as students follow along. Then, ask students (in pairs) to follow the basic steps you modeled with Sample C. *Working with partners,* they should:

- Talk about whether the author uses the word *nice* too much.
- Talk about other ways the writer could have said the same thing.
- Refer to the class brainstorming list *if they wish.*
- Revise by replacing the word *nice* one or more times.
- Read their revision aloud to each other—noticing the spice!

Step 6: Sharing and Discussing Results

When students have finished, ask several pairs of students to share their revisions aloud with the whole class. How many different ways did the class find to say *nice?*

Next Steps

- Encourage your students to keep a journal log of favorite words and to be frequent borrowers when it comes to language. When you share a book or poem aloud, you may wish to "capture" a favorite word and add it to a class list.

- Revise a piece of your own writing by finding another spicier way to say *nice.* You might wish to share two or three possibilities, and ask students to help you choose the one they think has the most spice and pizzazz.

- Continue to look and listen not only for ways to say *nice,* but ways authors describe things in general.
  Recommended:
  - *All Pigs Are Beautiful* by Dick King-Smith. 1993. Cambridge, MA: Candlewick Press.
  - *Big Blue Whale* by Nicola Davies. 1997. Cambridge, MA: Candlewick Press.
  - *Gentle Giant Octopus* by Karen Wallace. 1998. Cambridge, MA: Candlewick Press.
  - *Toad* by Ruth Brown. 1996. New York: Dutton Children's Books.

- *For students who need a challenge:* One of the most powerful ways to create a description is by making a comparison—creating a *simile,* in other words. In *Gentle Giant Octopus* (recommended list), Karen Wallace tells us that the mother octopus is "huge like a spaceship." She also tells us that her tentacles "fly like ribbons behind her" (page 6). Notice how vivid these descriptions are. Some of your students may be ready to try describing one thing by comparing it to another. A good way to begin is by asking, "What does it remind you of?" Comparative description adds power to writing.

Sample A

A Nice Picnic

Bethany had a party. Three of her friends came, and everyone had a really nice time. They ate hot dogs, watermelon, and cake. They drank lemonade. Everything tasted so nice. Bethany's dad put up a net in the back yard, and they had a nice time playing volleyball, batting the ball over the net.

Is <u>nice</u> used too much?

___ Yes!   ___ No

Sample B

The Gift

Carlos and Andre wanted to get a nice gift for Mrs. Ramirez, who lived on their street. They wanted to get her something special. Carlos thought of flowers. "Flowers are so beautiful," he said. But Andre had another idea. "Balloons would be even more terrific!" he said. "They cheer you up—and they don't need water!"

Is <u>nice</u> used too much?

___ Yes!   ___ No

Suggested Revision of Sample A

A ~~Nice~~ Super Picnic

Bethany had a party. Three of her friends came, and everyone had a really ~~nice~~ exciting time. They ate hot dogs, watermelon, and cake. They drank lemonade. Everything tasted ~~so nice~~ delicious. Bethany's dad put up a net in the back yard, and they had a ~~nice~~ wild time playing volleyball, batting the ball over the net.

Sample C: Whole Class Revision

Ms. Brown

Ms. Brown was a nice teacher. When one of her students had a hard time with reading or math, she would always find something nice to say. She also collected pennies. Every time she found one, she would put it in a "wish jar," and make a wish for her students. When they got 1,000 pennies, they would buy a class treat. Wasn't that a nice idea?

Sample D: Revising with Partners

Dinosaur Crazy

Dakota <u>loved</u> dinosaurs. She thought they were very nice. One day, Dakota got a nice surprise. Her grandma bought her a HUGE book about dinosaurs. Dakota could <u>not</u> stop reading that book! She thought it was really nice!

Suggested Revisions of C and D

Sample C: Whole Class Revision

Ms. Brown

Ms. Brown was a ~~nice~~ super teacher. When one of her students had a

hard time with reading or math, she would always find

something ~~nice~~ kind to say. She also collected pennies. Every time

she found one, she would put it in a "wish jar," and make a

wish for her students. When they got 1,000 pennies, they would

buy a class treat. Wasn't that a ~~nice~~ fabulous idea?

Sample D: Revising with Partners

Dinosaur Crazy

Dakota <u>loved</u> dinosaurs. She thought they were ~~very nice~~ fascinating. One

day, Dakota got a ~~nice~~ terrific surprise. Her grandma bought her a

HUGE book about dinosaurs. Dakota could <u>not</u> stop reading

that book! She thought it was really ~~nice~~ exciting!

Putting Capitals on Proper Names

Trait Connection: **Being an Editor (Conventions)**

Introduction (Share with students in your own words)

When you write your name, do you make the first letter a capital? Every single time? *Terrific.* That's a good way to let your reader know, "Hey—this is a name!" What *other* things have proper names—besides people? [Pause for discussion.]

Here are some we thought of. Did you think of all these? *Cities, states, countries, pets, streets, books, movies,* and *schools.* Those are just a FEW of the things that have names. Did you think of others? Remember—if it's a name (like Beatrice, Chicago, or Spiderman), it gets a capital letter, even if it isn't a *person's* name. Think how bad your goldfish Harvey would feel if you spelled his name with a small "h." (Especially if his name was really Fred.)

Names of everyday things—like *television, chair,* or *broccoli*—don't get a capital. It's easy to tell. Just try putting the word *the* or *a* in front of it. If you can, it *doesn't usually* get a capital: *the cat, a chair, the broccoli, a television.* No capitals. But it wouldn't make sense to say *a Chicago* or *the Beatrice.* See the difference?

Here's one easy way to put in a missing capital. Put a caret right below the small letter you want to change, and put in a capital right above it—like this:

Marie's cat T̂oby did NOT like getting shots.

Teaching the Lesson (General Guidelines for Teachers)

1. Remind students how to insert a missing capital by writing right over the lower case letter.

2. Practice putting capitals on names, using our example and several you make up.

3. Talk about names enough so that students feel comfortable with the concept of a name and know what *kinds* of names need a capital letter. (This skill takes time and even adults struggle with it—so having a good start at understanding is enough for now!)

4. Share the editing lesson on page 143. Read it aloud. The ONLY errors in this lesson are *four names missing a capital letter.*

5. Ask students to work individually first, then check with a partner. Remind them to look for names.

6. When everyone is done, ask them to *coach you* as you edit the copy on an overhead transparency.

7. When you finish, check your editing against the corrected copy.

Goal: Find 4 missing capitals on names.
Watch for names in your own writing—and mark them with capital letters.

Editing Practice

Add 4 capitals to names.

Little dinah was a monkey. She liked to

tease her trainer, alice, by hiding bananas

behind the sofa. Alice said Dinah was the

funniest monkey in san diego.

Corrected Copy

4 capitals on names inserted

Little **D**inah was a monkey. She liked to

tease her trainer, **A**lice, by hiding bananas

behind the sofa. Alice said Dinah was the

funniest monkey in **S**an **D**iego.

"Went" Needs to "Go"

Trait Connection: **Word Choice**

Introduction

Have you ever looked at two different pictures of yourself and thought, "Boy, I like this one a LOT better!"? Maybe it just looked more like the way you really see yourself. When writers revise, they aren't just changing words. They are changing the picture those words make in a reader's mind. In the last lesson, you looked for other ways to say something was *nice*. In this lesson, you'll have a chance to play with the word *went*. Ready? Let's see how clear we can make those pictures . . .

Teacher's Sidebar . . .

Good revision begins with the writer getting a picture in his or her own mind. It helps some students to just close their eyes and think for a minute. They might picture a dog plunging into a river, or a bird landing delicately on the edge of her nest. The more clearly they can see an event in their minds, the more likely it is they will come up with the right words to write about it.

Focus and Intent

This lesson is intended to help students:

- Explore different ways to say something.
- Think of alternatives for the word *went.*
- Revise a piece by finding new ways to express an idea.

Teaching the Lesson

Step 1: Getting Writers Thinking About Options

Give students some alternatives to *went* that they can act out. Write them on 3×5 cards, and do some quick coaching to make sure students know the meanings. (You may wish to have students work in teams of two.) Ask students to act out their words as the rest of the class tries to guess. As they come up with good guesses (right or not), record them. But, do let them know when they get the word right! Possibilities include *ran, marched, climbed, crept, crawled, hid, crouched, tiptoed, danced, skipped, rolled, bumped, jumped, fell, drove, biked, skated, swam, dove*, and *flew.*

Step 2: Making the Reading-Writing Connection

When the book *Verdi* opens, a mother python is sending her newly hatched little yellow snakes off into the jungle where they can grow into large, green pythons—just like her. One of them, Verdi, is hanging back—

> *But Verdi dawdled. He was proudly eyeing his bright yellow skin. He especially liked the bold stripes that zigzagged down his back. Why the hurry to grow up big and green? he wondered.*

(Janell Cannon. *Verdi*. 1997. New York: Harcourt Brace and Company. Unpaginated.)

Have you ever dawdled? If you have, you know it means to move really *slowly*—almost looking for excuses *not* to move. Instead of "dawdled," Janell Cannon might have written, "went slowly." Would that have been a good choice? Have you ever seen lightning zigzag through the sky? If you have, you know a zigzag whips one way—then suddenly shoots the other way. Instead of saying Verdi's stripes "zigzagged down his back," the author could have written that the stripes "*went* down his back." Which choice makes a better picture?

Step 3: Involving Students as Evaluators

Ask students to look at Samples A and B as you read them aloud, listening for the word *went*—and asking if one writer uses it a little too much. (At the bottom of each sample is a place to check "yes" or "no.") When you finish reading each sample, give students a minute to talk with a partner about whether there might be a better word than *went* to make a clear picture.

Discussing Results

Students will likely notice that the word *went* is used several times in Sample B—but not in A. Ask if anyone can think of another way to express some of the ideas in Sample B. Remind students that while there is nothing wrong with the word *went*, sometimes a different word makes a sharper picture. (If you wish, share our suggested revision for Sample B.)

Step 4: Modeling Revision

- Share Sample C (*Whole Class Revision*) with students. Read it aloud.
- Ask students to count how many times the word *went* is used. Is it too many? (Most should say *yes*.)
- Ask students for suggestions on "other ways to say it."
- Revise by replacing *went* one or more times with a different word or expression. Use your class list of alternatives, if you wish—or just brainstorm.
- When you finish, read your revision aloud. Did replacing *went* sharpen the picture? (*Optional:* Compare your revision with ours. Your copy *need not match ours.*)

Step 5: Revising with Partners

Share Sample D (*Revising with Partners*). Read it aloud as students follow along. Also read through the sidebar list of other words that could replace *went*. Add to this list *if you wish*. Then, ask students (in pairs) to follow the basic steps you modeled with Sample C. *Working with partners,* they should:

- Underline each instance of the word *went*.

- Talk about other words the writer *could* have used.

- Refer to the sidebar list of other words for *went*—or make up their own.

- Revise by replacing the word *went* one or more times.

- Read their revision aloud to each other.

Step 6: Sharing and Discussing Results

When students have finished, ask several pairs of students to share their revisions aloud with the whole class. How many different ways did the class find to say *went?* Did they sharpen the picture?

Next Steps

- Remind students to *double space* their writing—in case they ever need to replace one word with another.

- Revise a piece of your own writing by finding another way to say *went.* You might wish to share two or three possibilities, and ask students to help you choose the one they think creates the sharpest picture.

- Continue to look and listen for words that make clear pictures in the literature you share aloud. Recommended:

  - *Verdi* by Janell Cannon. 1997. New York: Harcourt Brace and Company.

  - *Amos and Boris* by William Steig. 1971. New York: Puffin Books.

  - *Crickwing* by Janell Cannon. 2000. New York: Harcourt Brace and Company.

  - *The Great Fuzz Frenzy* by Janet Stevens and Susan Stevens Crummel. 2005. New York: Harcourt Brace and Company.

- *For students who need a challenge:* Though we have focused on the word *went*, this is clearly a lesson on verbs. Some students may be ready to explore the notion of strong verbs—and their impact on writing—in a broader sense. A good way to begin is by creating a personal collection of favorite "motion" words, just jotting them down in a notebook. Students who do this should be allowed to choose a word now and then for the whole class to explore—with your help. You might define it, act it out, or create art to show the "snapshot" version of your special word in action.

Sample A

Bad Fall

Nikki was SO excited. Her dad was coming home. He was in the Army. She RACED down the hall and slipped on the wet floor. The janitor was cleaning the linoleum. Nikki's feet flew out from under her and she went sprawling. She tumbled down the hard stairs and crashed against the wall. OUCH!!!!

Is <u>went</u> used too much?

___ Yes!   ___ No

Sample B

The Race

Emile felt ready for the big race. When the coach nodded,

Emile went to the starting line. The whistle blew. Emile

took off. He went as fast as his legs would go! He went

over every hurdle! He went across the finish line—then

went down in a heap on the ground. He had WON!!!

Is <u>went</u> used too much?

__ Yes!   __ No

Suggested Revision of Sample B

The Race

Emile felt ready for the big race. When the coach nodded,

Emile ~~went~~ **walked** to the starting line. The whistle blew. Emile

took off. He ~~went~~ **ran** as fast as his legs would go! He ~~went~~ **leaped**

over every hurdle! He ~~went~~ **raced** across the finish line—then

~~went~~ **fell** down in a heap on the ground. He had WON!!!

Sample C: Whole Class Revision

Sly Octopus

An ENORMOUS crab went after a tiny octopus. The octopus went through the water, sending out jets of black ink. The crab went right after it! Finally, with the crab nipping at its arms, the octopus went under a low rock. The crab tried, but could not reach!

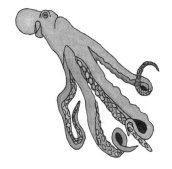

Sample D: Revising with Partners

Good Catch!

Sam took her dog Taffy to the park to play Frisbee. Sam threw the Frisbee. Taffy went after it. Sam threw again. The Frisbee went into the pond! No problem!! Taffy went in right after it. What a dog!!

went . . .
raced
tore
ran
jumped
leaped
sailed
flew

Suggested Revisions of C and D

Sample C: Whole Class Revision

Sly Octopus

An ENORMOUS crab ~~went~~ **swam** after a tiny octopus. The

octopus ~~went~~ **zoomed** through the water, sending out jets of black

ink. The crab ~~went~~ **scrambled** right after it! Finally, with the crab

nipping at its arms, the octopus ~~went~~ **hid** under a low rock. The

crab tried, but could not reach!

Sample D: Revising with Partners

Good Catch!

Sam took her dog Taffy to the park to play Frisbee. Sam

threw the Frisbee. Taffy ~~went~~ **tore** after it. Sam threw again. The

Frisbee ~~went~~ **sailed** into the pond! No problem!! Taffy ~~went~~ **jumped** in

right after it. What a dog!!

Random Capitals

Trait Connection: **Being an Editor (Conventions)**

Introduction (Share with students in your own words)

You've had a chance now to use capital letters for two things: (1) to begin a sentence, and (2) to show that a word is a name. So far, so good. But, did you know capital letters could be like mushrooms after it rains? Sometimes, they just pop up in the funniest places—like right in the middle of a word:

My cAt is hungry!

Oops! What's that capital A doing there? *Nothing*, really! Hey, here's another capital popping up like a mushroom on a word that isn't even a name:

We rode on the Bus.

Bus isn't a name, is it? No way. To get rid of these mushroomy capitals, an editor uses a little line called a slash mark. It looks like this: **/** A slash mark says, "Get down! Get down, you pesky capital! Become a little letter, like you're supposed to!" The slash mark goes right through the capital letter, like this:

My cAt is hungry!

We rode on the Bus.

Teaching the Lesson (General Guidelines for Teachers)

1. Show students how to make a slash mark: a little line angling down and left.
2. Practice turning capital letters into lower case letters by writing slash marks.
3. Talk about when and why writers use a capital letter. (Ongoing reminders may be needed for this, especially for students who are still distinguishing between capital and lower case letters. This lesson only makes an introduction.)
4. Share the editing lesson on the following page. Read it aloud. The ONLY errors in this lesson are *3 capital letters* that do not belong.
5. Ask students to work individually first, then check with a partner. Remind them to look for capital letters acting like mushrooms, popping up where they do not belong.
6. When everyone is done, ask them to *coach you* as you edit the copy on an overhead transparency.
7. When you finish, check your editing against the corrected copy.

Goal: Find 3 "mushrooming" capitals that don't belong.
Watch out for "mushrooms" in your own writing.

Editing Practice

Find 3 capitals that do not belong.

I like to ride the Bus. It is very Cool.

I always tRy to get the front seat.

Corrected Copy

3 capitals changed to small letters

I like to ride the Bus. It is very Cool.

I always try to get the front seat.

Revising with Shape, Size, and Color

Trait Connection: **Word Choice**

Introduction

Shape, size, and color are three VERY helpful ways of describing things. If you read that something is the shape of a doughnut, or the size of an elephant, or the color of the morning sun, you know just what the writer is talking about. In this lesson, you'll use details of shape, size, and color to create vivid pictures for your reader.

Teacher's Sidebar . . .
Sometimes writers just use *one word* to describe something: *The sky was <u>gray</u>*. Other times, one word isn't enough. They need to say more: *The sky was a dark gray like the inside of an old tin cup*. That's not just any old gray. It's a special kind of gray.

Focus and Intent

This lesson is intended to help students:

- Recognize the importance of description in good writing.
- Listen for details of size, shape, or color in literature shared aloud.
- Use details of size, shape, or color to revise a piece that has minimal description.

Teaching the Lesson

Step 1: Getting Writers Thinking About Shape, Size, and Color

The purpose of this lesson is to nudge students beyond broad descriptions like *big* or *brown* to something more precise. Warm up by coaching them (*How* big? What *shade* of brown?) to revise the following examples (the first three are done for you):

One Word	A Little More
tall	*ten feet high*
dark	*inky black with no light*
bright	*like sun shining on the sand*
big	_____
small	_____
blue	_____
red	_____

Step 2: Making the Reading-Writing Connection

In Cynthia Rylant's book *Scarecrow,* the main character—Scarecrow himself—is enchanted by the world around him. He loves the sun, the moon, the birds who land on his arms, and the children who come to plant—

Seeds are being planted, and inside them there are ten-foot-tall sunflowers and mammoth pumpkins and beans that just go on forever.

(Cynthia Rylant. *Scarecrow.* 1997. New York: Harcourt Brace and Company. Unpaginated.)

Most people know sunflowers are big. But *how big* does Cynthia Rylant make them? What special word for *big* does she use to describe the pumpkins? She could have said the children were planting seeds that would grow into "many, many beans." But she didn't. She found some other interesting words to use instead of "many." Do you remember what she wrote?

Step 3: Involving Students as Evaluators

Ask students to look at Samples A and B as you read them aloud, listening for words about shape, size, or color that help us make pictures in our minds. When you finish reading each sample, give students a minute to talk with a partner about whether the writer uses details about shape, size, or color to make a clear picture. (At the bottom of each sample is a place to check "yes" or "no.")

Discussing Results

Most students should find Sample B stronger. Ask if anyone can think of another way to express some of the ideas in Sample A. (If you wish, share our suggested revision for Sample A.)

Step 4: Modeling Revision

- Share Sample C (*Whole Class Revision*) with students. Read it aloud.
- Ask students whether the writer uses details about shape, size, and color to make a clear picture in our minds. (Most should say *no.*)
- Ask students for suggestions on adding shape, size, or color details to this piece. They might add a single word—e.g., *red*—or a whole descriptive line.
- Revise by inserting one or more descriptive details, using the caret.
- When you finish, read your revision aloud. Did your shape, size, and color details make the picture easier to see in your minds? (*Optional:* Compare your revision with ours. Your copy *need not match ours.*)

Step 5: Revising with Partners

Share Sample D (*Revising with Partners*). Read it aloud as students follow along. Then, ask students (in pairs) to follow the basic steps you modeled with Sample C.

Working with partners, they should:

- Talk about whether the writer uses details of shape, size, or color.

- Talk about details they could add.

- Insert any details they wish—from single words to whole phrases or sentences.

- Read their revision aloud to each other.

Step 6: Sharing and Discussing Results

When students have finished, ask several pairs of students to share their revisions aloud with the whole class. How many different details of shape, size, and color did your students come up with? Did they make it easier to picture what they were describing?

Next Steps

- Remind students to *double space* their writing—in case they ever need to add a detail of shape, size, or color.

- Revise a piece of your own writing by adding shape, size, or color details. Ask students to coach you as you work.

- Continue to look and listen for shape, size, and color details in the literature you share aloud.
  Recommended:
  - *Scarecrow* by Cynthia Rylant. 1997. New York: Harcourt Brace and Company.
  - *All the Colors of the Earth* by Sheila Hamanaka. 1994. New York: William Morrow and Company.
  - *Everybody Needs a Rock* by Byrd Baylor. 1974. New York: Aladdin Books.
  - *In Daddy's Arms I Am Tall: African Americans Celebrating Fathers* by Javaka Steptoe, illustrator. Individual poets. 1997. New York: Lee and Low Books, Inc.
  - *Tigress* by Dick Dowson. 2004. Cambridge, MA: Candlewick Press.

- *For students who need a challenge:* Sometimes it's fun to name the details first—and leave the thing being described a mystery until the very last line. Students can begin with a list of details covering shape, size, and color—or anything else. Then, they can transform the list into a poem, one or two details per line. The last line of the poem reveals what the poet is describing!

Sample A

Yum!

Nico wanted something to drink. Nana

stirred some powder into warm milk and

poured it into a cup. On top, she floated a

marshmallow. The marshmallow melted.

Details of shape, size, and color?

___ Yes!   ___ No

Sample B

Brrrrrrrr!!

When Jacob poked his nose out the door, it turned bright pink in the cold air. "Brrrr!" he said, tugging his red hat down over his ears. The hat poked out on both sides, like a cow with short, fuzzy horns. Jacob took off through the glittery snow, making a blue shadow and leaving a long winding river of footprints.

Details of shape, size, and color?

___ Yes!   ___ No

Suggested Revision of Sample A

Yum!

Nico wanted something to drink. Nana

chocolate brown

stirred some ^powder into warm milk and

giant purple   *fat*

poured it into a ^cup. On top, she floated a ^

the size of a golf ball.

marshmallow ^. The marshmallow melted ^

into the shape of a dinosaur's head.

Sample C: Whole Class Revision

Building a Home

All morning, the robin was busy, building, building, building. It gathered twigs. It gathered grass. It scooped up some mud. It used the mud to shape its nest. When the nest was done, the robin lined it with feathers.

Sample D: Revising with Partners

Storm on the Lake

Before a storm hits, a lake is calm. The top of the lake is smooth. As the storm moves in, the lake turns a different color. Waves get big.

Suggested Revisions of C and D

Sample C: Whole Class Revision

Building a Home

All morning, the robin was busy, building,

building, building. It gathered ^thin, green^ twigs. It gathered

^dry, brown^ grass. It scooped up some ^thick^ mud. It used the mud

to shape its nest. ^like a shallow bowl.^ When the nest was done, the

robin lined it with ^tiny, gray and white^ feathers.

Sample D: Revising with Partners

Storm on the Lake

Before a storm hits, a lake is calm. The top of

the lake is smooth. ^like a blue mirror.^ As the storm moves in, the

lake turns ^as gray and brown as mud.^ ~~a different color.~~ Waves get ~~big.~~ ^two feet high.^

Capital "I"

Trait Connection: **Being an Editor (Conventions)**

Introduction (Share with students in your own words)

Every person has a name—and that name always starts with a capital letter, right? Right. Writers don't always refer to themselves using their names, of course. It would sound too weird. If your name were Fred, you wouldn't say to someone, "Fred is hungry. Fred needs a sandwich!" What *would* you say? *I*, of course! You'd say, "*I* am hungry! *I* need a sandwich—*please!*" (Writers should always be polite.) When you refer to yourself as "I," it's still a kind of name, and it still needs a capital letter. Is "I" capitalized every time? Yes—every single time. It's less confusing that way. So, how many capital "I's" would you need in these two sentences?

- i think i just saw a bear!
- If i think of it, i will phone you.

If you said *one,* take another look. If you said *two,* look closer. If you said *three,* you're doing some good editing—but you still missed something. Read the sentences one more time. If you said *four,* you are an editing champ today. Now, do you remember how to turn a lower case letter into a capital? Insert a caret, and write the capital just above it—like this:

- I think I just saw a bear!
- If I think of it, I will phone you.

Teaching the Lesson (General Guidelines for Teachers)

1. Remind students how to insert a capital (with a caret).
2. Practice turning a lower case "i" into a capital "I," using our examples or your own. Remind students that "I" is a kind of name.
3. Share the editing lesson on the following page. Read it aloud. The ONLY errors in this lesson are *3 missing capital I's.*
4. Ask students to work individually first, then check with a partner. Remind them to look for 3 *I's* that need to be capitalized.
5. When everyone is done, ask them to *coach you* as you edit the copy on an overhead transparency.
6. When you finish, check your editing against the corrected copy.

Goal: Change three lower case "i's" into capitals.
Look for "I" in your own work—and make sure it's a capital!

Editing Practice

Change small "i" to capital "I" 3 times.

i love the city. Sometimes when I walk

through the city, i smell popcorn or

doughnuts. If I have a dollar with me, i

might buy a snack!

Corrected Copy

3 capital "I's" inserted

I love the city. Sometimes when I walk

through the city, I smell popcorn or

doughnuts. If I have a dollar with me, I

might buy a snack!

Revising by Building Longer Sentences

Trait Connection: **Sentence Fluency**

Introduction

Writers sometimes use tiny sentences: *It was cold*. And sometimes they write rather long sentences: *Even with his mittens and hat, even with his jacket buttoned right up to the top button and his ears wrapped in a woolly scarf, Nick still felt chilly*. Tiny sentences are tiny because—usually—they just hold one idea. Longer sentences hold more ideas. When writers build longer sentences out of tiny ones, they can share more than one idea at a time.

Teacher's Sidebar . . .
Short sentences have power. We do NOT want to eliminate them! At the same time, sentence combining builds thinking skills. Each time a writer adds one more thought, one more idea, he or she must think about where that idea fits—and whether adding it means beginning the sentence differently.

Focus and Intent

This lesson is intended to help students:

- Understand that bigger sentences can be built out of small ones.
- Listen for all the different ideas expressed within a single sentence.
- Revise by combining tiny sentences into one longer sentence.

Teaching the Lesson

Step 1: Getting Writers Thinking About Combining

Sentence combining is a critical writing skill, one that's built over *years* of practice. Eventually, your student writers will be able to combine fairly lengthy or complex sentences. For now, we want to introduce the idea that a writer can *sometimes* put more than one idea into a single sentence. Share the following examples with students to see if they can combine two ideas into one sentence. Ask, "How could we put these two ideas into one sentence?" Make up an additional example or two if you feel they need more practice. The first two are done for you as models.

1. *Two tiny sentences:*
   A bird flew by. It was blue.

   Combined: **A blue bird flew by.**

2. *Two tiny sentences:*
   A dog barked. He barked loudly.

   Combined: **A dog barked loudly.**

3. *Two tiny sentences:*
   The wind blew. It blew hard.

   Combined: _____ .

4. *Two tiny sentences:*
   Jon was running. He was running down the road.

   Combined: _____ .

Step 2: Making the Reading-Writing Connection

William Steig's book, *Doctor DeSoto,* opens with a sentence that contains several different ideas. Listen and see if you can remember all the different things this writer tells us in just one sentence:

> *Doctor DeSoto, the dentist, did very good work, so he had no end of patients.*
>
> (William Steig. *Doctor DeSoto.* 1982. New York: Farrar, Straus and Giroux. Unpaginated.)

Listen to the sentence again. How many different ideas are there? [Pause for response. Write the sentence out, if you wish.] We learn that Doctor DeSoto was a dentist (that's one idea), he did good work (two), and he had "no end of patients" (three). So, if William Steig were writing this book *all* in tiny sentences, how many would he need just for those three ideas?

Step 3: Involving Students as Evaluators

Ask students to look at Samples A and B as you read them aloud, listening for ideas and noticing how many ideas are in one sentence. When you finish reading each sample, give students a minute to talk with a partner about whether the writer uses tiny sentences or longer sentences (with more than one idea in a sentence). (At the bottom of each sample is a place to check "yes" or "no.")

Discussing Results

Most students should hear longer sentences in Sample A, and tiny sentences in Sample B. Ask if anyone can think of a way to combine any of the sentences in Sample B. (If you wish, share our suggested revision for Sample B.)

Step 4: Modeling Revision

- Share Sample C (*Whole Class Revision*) with students. Read it aloud more than once.

- Ask students whether the writer uses tiny sentences. (Most should say *yes.*)

- Ask students for suggestions on combining *any* of the sentences. They might combine just one set of two, or combine more than that.

- Revise by combining two or more sentences, using the delete sign and caret or other editorial marks as needed.

- When you finish, read your revision aloud. Were you able to create a sentence with more than one idea? (*Optional:* Compare your revision with ours. Your copy *need not match ours.*)

Step 5: Revising with Partners

Share Sample D (*Revising with Partners*). Read it aloud (more than once) as students follow along. Then, ask students (in pairs) to follow the basic steps you modeled with Sample C. *Working with partners,* they should:

- Talk about whether the writer writes in tiny sentences.
- Talk about sentences that could be combined.
- Combine any two sentences—or more.
- Read their revision aloud to each other.

Step 6: Sharing and Discussing Results

When students have finished, ask several pairs of students to share their revisions aloud with the whole class. How many different ideas did writing teams put into one sentence?

Next Steps

- Remind students to *read their own writing aloud* after they write—in case they decide to put two sentences together.

- Revise a piece of your own writing by combining sentences. Ask students to coach you as you work.

- Pause occasionally to listen for the number of different ideas writers put into one sentence in the literature you share aloud.
  Recommended:

  - *Doctor DeSoto* by William Steig. 1982. New York: Farrar, Straus and Giroux.

  - *Amos and Boris* by William Steig. 1977. New York: Puffin Books.

- *The Relatives Came* by Cynthia Rylant. 1985. New York: Aladdin Paperbacks.

- *What Do You Do When Something Wants to Eat You?* by Steve Jenkins. 1997. Boston: Houghton Mifflin.

■ *For students who need a challenge:* For students who are ready, try a game that is fun to play with teams of two or three. Ask the team to combine two sentences. Then, add a third. Can they weave that in to make one big sentence? If they are ready—add a fourth! Keep going until they cannot do more. If you like, turn the tables and let them challenge you by giving you two tiny sentences, then a third, fourth, and so on. You can also challenge writers by giving them a long or complex sentence from any piece of literature and asking them to take it apart into a series of tiny sentences.

Sample A

Stars

If you look up into the sky on a crystal clear night, you might see about 2,000 stars. Of course, if you have a small telescope, you will see even more. And if you have a BIG telescope, you might see <u>millions</u> of stars. If there are so many stars, why don't we see them during the daytime? Don't worry. They are still there, but the sun is so bright the stars are invisible.

___ Tiny sentences with one idea each?

___ Bigger sentences with more than one idea?

Sample B

Hooray for Plants!

Plants give off oxygen. We breathe oxygen. Plants give food to humans. Plants give food to animals. Humans need plants to live. Animals need plants to live.

___ Tiny sentences with one idea each?

___ Bigger sentences with more than one idea?

Suggested Revision of Sample B

Hooray for Plants!

Plants give off oxygen. *that* We breathe ⊙ ~~oxygen.~~ Plants give

food to humans. ~~Plants give food~~ *and* to animals. Humans ~~need~~

~~plants to live.~~ *and* Animals need plants to live.

Sample C: Whole Class Revision

Recipe for Dirt

Dirt is made of tiny rocks. It contains tiny bits of dead plants. It contains tiny bits of dead animals. It even contains bacteria. It even contains air. It even contains water.

Sample D: Revising with Partners

The BIG Ride

Earth is moving. It is moving through space.

We don't feel it move. That's because the

ride is very smooth.

Suggested Revisions of C and D

Sample C: Whole Class Revision

Recipe for Dirt

Dirt is made of tiny rocks, ~~It contains~~ tiny

and

bits of dead plants, ~~It contains~~ tiny bits of

dead animals. It even contains bacteria, ~~It~~

and

~~even contains~~ air, ~~It even contains~~ water.

Sample D: Revising with Partners

The BIG Ride

Earth is moving ~~It is moving~~ through space.

We don't feel it move ~~That's~~ because the

ride is very smooth.

All About Capitals

Trait Connection: **Being an Editor (Conventions)**

Introduction (Share with students in your own words)

As an editor, you have put in missing capitals to begin a sentence or to show that a word, including "I," is a name. You've slashed out capitals that popped up like mushrooms when they weren't needed. In this lesson, you'll have a chance to put everything you know about editing capitals into practice all at once, so let's review. What would you do with each of these sentences?

- my friend fell off his bike!
- A big Storm blew through our town.
- i wonder where amy left the basketball.

If you said Sentence 1 needs to begin with a capital, your editorial skills are sharp today. If you said Sentence 2 needs a slash right through the capital S in *Storm*, you are definitely an editor on the lookout. And if you spotted the missing capitals on the name *Amy* and on *I*, you have four for four. Editing doesn't get better than that. Do you remember how to make these corrections? Just like this—

- **M**y friend fell off his bike!
- A big $torm blew through our town.
- I wonder where **A**my left the basketball.

Teaching the Lesson (General Guidelines for Teachers)

1. Remind students how to insert a capital (caret and capital above) or turn a capital into a lower case letter (with a slash mark).
2. Practice inserting capitals or turning capitals into lower case letters, using our examples or your own. Talk about the reason behind each correction.
3. Share the editing lesson on the following page. Read it aloud. The ONLY errors in this lesson are *3 missing capitals and one popping up where it doesn't belong.*
4. Ask students to work individually first, then check with a partner. Remind them to look for 4 errors.
5. When everyone is done, ask them to *coach you* as you edit the copy on an overhead transparency.
6. When you finish, check your editing against the corrected copy.

Goal: Correct 4 errors with capitals.
Look for missing capitals—or unneeded capitals—in your own work.

Editing Practice

4 errors with capitals

My best friend jamila rode her Bike to my

house. i was so happy to see her! we rode

bikes all day.

Corrected Copy

4 errors with capitals corrected

My best friend Jamila rode her Bike to my house. I was so happy to see her! We rode bikes all day.

Revising by Finishing Sentences

Lesson 28

Trait Connection: **Sentence Fluency**

Introduction

A fragment is a *little piece* of a bigger sentence. We might think of it as a sentence that isn't finished yet—like socks without shoes, or a cone with no ice cream in it. Some fragments make sense: *Big deal. Sure thing. No way. Good job!* [You may wish to write these out so students can see them.] You have probably used one or more of those fragments yourself. But what about this one: *Mark saw.* Does that make sense? No. Why not? [Pause for responses.] We don't know who or what Mark saw. Good writers are careful to finish *most* of their sentences so they make sense. In this lesson, you'll get practice doing that.

Teacher's Sidebar . . .

Good writers use fragments all the time. You may find that your student writers—young though they are—sometimes use fragments quite effectively because it's a natural way of speaking in American English. There is nothing wrong with this—and you should *not* feel compelled to make them correct every fragment. What's important is to make sure students understand the difference between a fragment and a whole sentence—and know how to turn one into the other.

Focus and Intent

This lesson is intended to help students:

- Understand what a fragment is.
- Distinguish between whole sentences and fragments.
- Revise by finishing a sentence to make it complete.

Teaching the Lesson

Step 1: Getting Writers Thinking About Fragments

Finishing sentences is fairly easy once you understand the difference between a fragment (a piece of a sentence) and a whole sentence. Hearing the difference takes practice—more than you can provide in one lesson. This lesson makes a beginning; you can provide further instruction through more examples—recognizing that this is a skill students will practice throughout their writing lives. For now, warm up by giving students examples and asking them, "Is this a piece of a sentence (a fragment), or a whole sentence with a *whole idea?*" For each fragment (Examples 2, 4 and 5), ask students to help you make a whole idea by adding the words you need.

1. Ben hit a home run.

2. Ravi found.

3. It rained all day.

4. The sun.

5. Broke the window.

Step 2: Making the Reading-Writing Connection

Sometimes writers use fragments on purpose. Really? Yes. This is very different from *forgetting* to finish a sentence—or just writing so fast you put the period in before the sentence is ready for it. So—why would a writer who *knows better* use a fragment on purpose? One answer is that fragments get a reader's attention. Here are a few that do that: *Wow! No kidding! Ouch!! Really? Splash! Finally! Good grief!* In a book called *Zomo The Rabbit*, writer Gerald McDermott uses two fragments and three sentences to introduce us to Zomo. See if you can tell which are which:

> *Zomo!*
> *Zomo the rabbit.*
> *He is not big.*
> *He is not strong.*
> *But he is very clever.*

(Gerald McDermott. *Zomo The Rabbit: A Trickster Tale from West Africa*. 1996. New York: Voyager Books. Unpaginated.)

Which ones were sentences? [Pause for response.] If you said the last three, you are right. The first two lines are fragments. Read them out loud. Why do you think Gerald McDermott uses these fragments on the very first page?

Step 3: Involving Students as Evaluators

Ask students to look at Samples A and B as you read them aloud, listening for fragments. When you finish reading each sample, give students a minute to talk with a partner about whether the writer uses fragments or not. (At the bottom of each sample is a place to check "yes" or "no.")

Discussing Results

Most students should hear fragments in Sample A, and none in Sample B. (If you wish, share our suggested revision for Sample A.)

Step 4: Modeling Revision

- Share Sample C (*Whole Class Revision*) with students. Read it aloud more than once.

- Ask students whether the writer uses fragments. (Most should say *yes.*)

- Ask students if they think any of the fragments in Sample C were included on purpose. *One* was (*Yuck!*)—and it does not need revision.

- Ask students for suggestions on finishing the other fragment.

- Revise by finishing that fragment, using a caret to insert needed words.

- When you finish, read your revision aloud. Does every sentence contain a whole idea now? (*Optional:* Compare your revision with ours. Your copy *need not match ours.*)

Step 5: Revising with Partners

Share Sample D (*Revising with Partners*). Read it aloud (more than once) as students follow along. Then, ask students (in pairs) to follow the basic steps you modeled with Sample C. *Working with partners,* they should:

- Talk about whether the writer uses any fragments.

- Talk about ways to finish any fragment they find (there is *one*).

- Finish the fragment by adding any words they like.

- Read their revision aloud to each other.

Step 6: Sharing and Discussing Results

When students have finished, ask several pairs of students to share their revisions aloud with the whole class. How many different ways did writing teams find to turn a fragment into a sentence?

Next Steps

- Remind students to *read their own writing aloud* after they write—listening for any fragments they did not create *on purpose.*

- Revise a piece of your own writing by finishing fragments to create whole sentences. Ask students to coach you as you work.

- Provide additional practice in distinguishing between sentences and fragments, keeping examples very easy at first.

- Pause occasionally to ask whether professional writers are using whole sentences or fragments. If they are using a fragment, ask students if they think it was on purpose. (Do not expect them to get this question right at first; with practice, they will.)

Recommended:

- *Zomo The Rabbit: A Trickster Tale from West Africa* by Gerald McDermott. 1996. New York: Voyager Books.

- *Aaaarrgghh! Spider!* by Lydia Monks. 2004. Boston: Houghton Mifflin.

- *Diary of a Wombat* by Jackie French. 2002. New York: Clarion Books.

- *Dogteam* by Gary Paulsen. 1994. New York: Dragonfly Books.

- *Don't Let the Pigeon Drive the Bus* by Mo Willems. 2003. New York: Hyperion Books for Children.

- *Knuffle Bunny* by Mo Willems. 2004. New York: Hyperion Books for Children.

- *For students who need a challenge:* Ask students who need a challenge to help you create some fragment strips. Simply print (in big letters) the first part of a (short) sentence on one strip . . . and the second part on another. You might use sentences from a favorite book as models. Only the first part will have a capital to begin. Only the second part will have ending punctuation. When you finish your set, pass out the strips randomly to other students in the class. See if students can find their sentence partners! (You can coach, of course.)

Sample A

Amazing Snow Flakes

Snow flakes are made of ice. They form in

clouds. Snow flakes start as small crystals.

The cold air. When they get heavy.

Fragments?

___ Yes!   ___ No

Sample B

Lightning

Lightning can be dangerous. It usually hits

tall things, like buildings or trees. If you see

lightning, go inside. If you can't go in, lie

flat in a low spot. Stay away from trees!

Fragments?

___ Yes!   ___ No

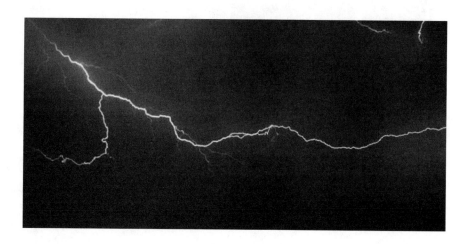

Suggested Revision of Sample A

Amazing Snow Flakes

Snow flakes are made of ice. They form in

clouds. Snow flakes start as small crystals.
makes them grow bigger.
The cold air. When they get heavy,
∧
they fall to the ground.

Sample C: Whole Class Revision

Smog

Smog is part smoke and part fog. Smog comes from dust in the air. It also comes from soot, smoke, and car exhaust. Yuck! Smog is not good for.

Sample D: Revising with Partners

Narrow Escape!

A parrot was sitting on a branch. A HUGE

cat came along! The parrot.

Suggested Revisions of C and D

Sample C: Whole Class Revision

Smog

Smog is part smoke and part fog. Smog

comes from dust in the air. It also comes

from soot, smoke, and car exhaust. Yuck!

Smog is not good for. *people to breathe.*
ə^

Sample D: Revising with Partners

Narrow Escape!

A parrot was sitting on a branch. A HUGE

cat came along! The parrot *took off like a rocket!*
ə^

Putting It Together
(All Editing Lessons)

Trait Connection: **Being an Editor (Conventions)**

Introduction (Share with students in your own words)

By now, you're probably beginning to feel like an editor. Like any good editor, you make choices—and changes: turning a lower case letter into a capital or deciding to use an exclamation point instead of a period. Because you're an editor on the lookout, you might catch a capital letter sneaking in where it doesn't belong—or a lower case *i* where a capital *I* should be.

In these lessons, you'll get four chances to put ALL your editing skills together. Each time you edit, you'll be looking for 5 different places where you can make good editing choices. You're the one with the pen—so you're in charge!

Teaching the Lesson (General Guidelines for Teachers)

1. Split this four-part lesson into four summary lessons, and do a different one each day. Review *only those specific skills* you need for the lesson at hand.
2. For each lesson, practice using any editorial marks your students will need: caret (∧), delete mark (⌀), caret with pound sign to insert space (#), and so on. Use examples from previous lessons or make up your own. Be sure to edit *with students so they can see just how it is done and copy you.*
3. Share the editing lessons on the following pages *one at a time.* These are different from preceding lessons because students will be looking for more than one kind of error at a time. Each lesson reinforces skills from previous lessons; no new skills are introduced.
4. As you begin each lesson, read the text aloud slowly and with expression so it is easy for students to hear where sentences end, which ones are questions, and so on. The kinds of errors are different in each of the three lessons, but in each lesson there are *5 errors.*
5. Ask students to work individually first, then check with a partner. Remind them to look and listen for 5 errors. If they get stuck, encourage them to read aloud softly.
6. When everyone is done editing, ask students to *coach you* as you edit the copy on an overhead transparency.
7. When you finish, check your editing against the corrected copy. Celebrate each error your students are able to correct on their own—even if they do not find all 5. Second graders are young editors, but many will surprise you with the numbers of errors they can find on their own. This is NOT a test. It is practice, and any lesson can be repeated.

Editing Practice Lesson #1

5 errors
___ **missing words**
___ **repeated words**
___ **words run together**

Tom could not wait the fair. He so excited.

The first thing he wanted to do was was ride

the roller coaster. He was not not one bit

scared! This would befun!!

Corrected Copy Lesson #1

✓ **2 missing words inserted**
✓ **2 repeated words deleted**
✓ **words run together split**

Tom could not wait ^for^ the fair. He ^was^ so excited.

The first thing he wanted to do was ~~was~~ ride

the roller coaster. He was not ~~not~~ one bit

scared! This would be fun!!

Editing Practice Lesson #2

5 errors
___ **missing periods (or exclamation points)**
___ **missing question marks**

Luis was helping Nana with the family

picnic He was in charge of tamales and cake

What a great picnic this would be Would

people say his cake was the best ever Would

Nana let him help again next year

Corrected Copy Lesson #2

✓ **3 missing periods (or exclamation points) inserted**
✓ **2 missing question marks inserted**

Luis was helping Nana with the family

picnic⊙ He was in charge of tamales and cake⊙
      ^   ^
                                            !
What a great picnic this would be^ Would
                                  ?
people say his cake was the best ever^ Would
                                      ?
Nana let him help again next year^
                                 ^

Editing Practice Lesson #3

5 errors
___ **spelling**
___ **capital "I"**

■ **what**
■ **when**
■ **where**

Mario asked me to play soccer wen we went

to the park. I said sure because i love soccer.

I don't know wat happened. I kicked the ball

SO hard, i couldn't see were it landed. We

never did find it!

Corrected Copy Lesson #3

✓ **3 spelling errors corrected**
✓ **2 capital "I" errors corrected**

- **what**
- **when**
- **where**

Mario asked me to play soccer ~~wen~~ *when* we went

to the park. I said sure because ~~i~~ I love soccer.

I don't know ~~wat~~ *what* happened. I kicked the ball

SO hard, ~~i~~ I couldn't see ~~were~~ *where* it landed. We

never did find it!

Editing Practice Lesson #4

5 errors
___ **capital to begin a sentence**
___ **capital on a name**
___ **capital not needed**
___ **missing question mark**
___ **missing period (or exclamation point)**

Do you like visiting the dentist It was time

for my checkup. I like Dr. mason, but

sometimes I get Worried. what if I have a

cavity? Luckily, this time I was fine

Corrected Copy Lesson #4

Corrected:
- ✓ **1 capital to begin a sentence**
- ✓ **1 capital on a name**
- ✓ **1 capital not needed**
- ✓ **1 missing question mark**
- ✓ **1 missing period (or exclamation point)**

Do you like visiting the dentist? It was time

for my checkup. I like Dr. Mason, but

sometimes I get Worried. What if I have a

cavity? Luckily, this time I was fine.

Revising to Show *Where*

Trait Connection: **Sentence Fluency**

Introduction

Little phrases that tell "where" can make writing very interesting. For instance, take this sentence: *Ted ran.* That's one whole idea—but, wouldn't we like to know more? We might like to know *where* Ted ran. Look how interesting we can make this sentence by using one—or more—phrases that tell *where: Ted ran . . . down the path . . . over the bridge . . . through the bushes . . . and into a bear!* There. Now, *that* was a more interesting run!! In this lesson, you'll revise some sentences to make them show *where*. By the way, where do you suppose Ted went next?

Teacher's Sidebar . . .

This is a lesson about prepositional phrases—but the good news is, you don't need to call them that to teach them. You can just call them little words that let writers show *where* something is happening. A few of these words are *in, across, by, around, behind, below, inside, on, near, over, under,* and *through*. As this lesson shows, little words can make a BIG difference when it comes to making sentences clear—and interesting.

Focus and Intent

This lesson is intended to help students:

- Understand how useful prepositional phrases can be (even though we won't call them by that name in this lesson!).
- Listen, in literature shared aloud, for phrases that show *where*.
- Revise a piece by adding phrases that show *where*.

Teaching the Lesson

Step 1: Getting Writers Thinking About <u>Where</u>

Prepositional phrases do more than show *where*, of course, but to keep this lesson simple, we'll focus on that one function—and instead of using the term *prepositional phrases*, we'll talk about *using little words to show where* something is happening: *under* the table, *over* the roof, *in* the lake. To get students warmed up, try acting out as many *where* phrases as you can, making a list of the small words (prepositions) as you go. (Write them in big print, so your students can refer to them later.) Begin by asking a simple question: *Where am I?* Act out the answer, asking students to describe where you are: *behind* the desk, *on* the chair, *in* the doorway. Ask students to act out as many as they can think of: *by* the window, *on* the rug, *under* a table, *near* the books, *in* the reading area, *under* the light, and so on. If you have a chance to do this outside, you can get even more creative!

Step 2: Making the Reading-Writing Connection

In Nicola Davies' book, *Bat Loves the Night*, Bat awakens to find herself hanging upside down. She doesn't stay on her perch long, though, for she loves to fly. And fly she does—but *where?* Listen, as the author uses little words to tell us:

> *Over bushes, under trees, between fence posts, through the tangled hedge she swoops untouched.*

> (Nicola Davies. *Bat Loves the Night.* 2004. Cambridge, MA: Candlewick. Page 12.)

In this small passage, the author gives us four "where" details. How many can you remember? [Pause for response—then read the passage aloud again, slowly, as students count them off. You may wish to have students stand and act these "where" phrases out as they listen.]

Step 3: Involving Students as Evaluators

Ask students to look at Samples A and B as you read them aloud, listening for phrases that tell us "where" something is happening. When you finish reading each sample, give students a minute to talk with a partner about whether the writer tells us *where*—or not. (At the bottom of each sample is a place to check "yes" or "no.")

Discussing Results

Most students should notice that Sample A tells *where*, while Sample B does not. Ask students if they can think of any opportunities in Sample B for the writer to tell us *where* something was happening. (If you wish, share our suggested revision for Sample B.)

Step 4: Modeling Revision

- Share Sample C (*Whole Class Revision*) with students. Read it aloud more than once.
- Ask students whether this writer tells us *where* the butterflies go. (Most should say *no.*)
- Ask students for suggestions on showing *where*.
- Revise by using prepositional phrases to show *where* the butterflies go.

- When you finish, read your revision aloud. Do the little added details give a bigger, more interesting picture? (*Optional:* Compare your revision with ours. Your copy *need not match ours*.)

Step 5: Revising with Partners

Share Sample D (*Revising with Partners*). Read it aloud (more than once) as students follow along. Then, ask students (in pairs) to follow the basic steps you modeled with Sample C. *Working with partners,* they should:

- Talk about whether the writer uses phrases that show *where*.
- Talk about ways to add *where* details.
- Revise by adding one or more phrases that show *where* a new puppy might go.
- Read their revision aloud to each other.

Step 6: Sharing and Discussing Results

When students have finished, ask several pairs of students to share their revisions aloud with the whole class. How many different places did writing teams have their puppies going?

Next Steps

- Remind students to *double space their drafts*—in case they decide to add a phrase showing *where*.

- Revise a piece of your own writing by adding one or more prepositional phrases to show *where*. Ask students to coach you, recommending as many possibilities as they can think of.

- Next time you take a field trip—or even go to the gym or soccer field or out for recess—practice using prepositional phrases to show just where the action occurred! Encourage students to think "where" when visiting a grocery store or a friend's house, or when riding in the car or on the bus. Thinking "where" makes writing "where" more natural.

- Pause occasionally to notice professional writers' use of prepositional phrases to show *where*. Write a few favorite sentences (chosen by students themselves) on the board for student writers to use as models.
  Recommended:

  - *Bat Loves the Night* by Nicola Davies. 2004. Cambridge, MA: Candlewick.

  - *The Night I Followed the Dog* by Nina Laden. 1994. San Francisco: Chronicle Books.

- *The Polar Express* by Chris Van Allsburg. 1985. Boston: Houghton Mifflin.
- *Stop That Pickle!* by Peter Armour. 1993. Boston: Houghton Mifflin.
- *That's Good! That's Bad!* by Margery Cuyler. 1991. New York: Henry Holt and Company.

■ *For students who need a challenge:* Prepositional phrases can pop up anywhere in a sentence—first, last, or in the middle. Putting them first, though, creates a special kind of suspense. Nicola Davies creates this suspense with her sentence from *Bat Loves the Night*. Look at it again, and notice how she saves the subject and verb for last. This gives her sentence both suspense and power. Ask students who need a challenge to use this sentence as a model. First, ask them to think of something or someone in motion—*anything* from a soccer ball or player to a space shuttle or astronaut will work. Second, ask them to think of at least three phrases to describe *where* the thing or person moves. Finally, using Nicola Davies' sentence as a model, ask them to write the *where* details first (prepositional phrases), and the *what* (subject and verb) last. It's fun to create a mystery in a single sentence! (For another masterful example of this technique see Gary Paulsen, *Dogteam*. 1993. New York: Delacorte Press.)

Sample A

Beaver Hideout

Beyond the houses, over a small hill, in the farthest corner of a tiny pond, lived a beaver family. The beaver father and mother spent their time building a beaver dam. Their five kits spent their days splashing in the water, chasing each other through the rushes, between the rocks, over the dam, and into the trees.

Tells where?

___ Yes!　　　___ No

Sample B

Hide and Seek

Francie and her friends Meko and Alfie were playing hide and seek. It was Alfie's turn to be "it." When Alfie closed his eyes, Francie and Meko ran! After counting to ten, Alfie looked. But he could not find them.

Tells where?

___ Yes!   ___ No

Suggested Revision of Sample B

Hide and Seek

Francie and her friends Meko and Alfie were

playing hide and seek. It was Alfie's turn to

be "it." When Alfie closed his eyes, Francie

and Meko ran. *around the corner and into the bushes!* After counting to ten, Alfie

looked. *under the porch and even in the trash can!* But he could not find them.

Sample C: Whole Class Revision

It Worked!

Students in Golden Valley School planted a butterfly garden. Then they waited for the butterflies to hatch—and discover their flowers. One day Maria looked out the window and announced, "They're here!" Butterflies were flying all over.

Sample D: Revising with Partners

New Puppy

Did you ever bring a new puppy home? If

you ever do, you could be in for a surprise!

Before you can blink, that puppy will go all

over.

Suggested Revisions of C and D

Sample C: Whole Class Revision

It Worked!

Students in Golden Valley School planted a

butterfly garden. Then they waited for the

butterflies to hatch—and discover their

flowers. One day Maria looked out the

window and announced, "They're here!"

Butterflies were flying ~~all over~~ *above the flowers, between the*

bushes, and all around the garden!

Sample D: Revising with Partners

New Puppy

Did you ever bring a new puppy home? If

you ever do, you could be in for a surprise!

Before you can blink, that puppy will go
~~all over~~ a ^ in the door, across the rug, onto the couch, into your bedroom, and through all your toys!